Praise for *The Perfect (Ofsted) Science Lesson*

Excellent ideas and practical tips on how to make this core subject manageable alongside an already over-crowded curriculum. The ideas about running science alongside the maths and English curriculum are well thought out and meet Ofsted's demands for a truly integrated curriculum that combines knowledge and skills equally.

Lucy Westley, AST in maths and assessment

An essential read for all training science teachers. A toolkit with ideas to try out – really useful for trainees hungry for suggestions. I like how it relates to metacognition and the use of learning conversations in relation to peer assessment. This book makes good reference to the relevant literature, whilst making it accessible. It also highlights the important of science in society and positive role models to make it relevant.

Dr Jo Anna Reed Johnson, University of Warwick

The useful and informative guidance in this book should form part of the armoury of all teachers who want to ensure that they deliver effective, informative and enjoyable science lessons. It clearly demonstrates not only the knowledge delivery but also the strategies that practitioners can employ to make learning enjoyable and relevant to their students, regardless of age.

Ian Fergus, Ofsted Inspector and former Head Teacher

THE PERFECT
SCIENCE
LESSON

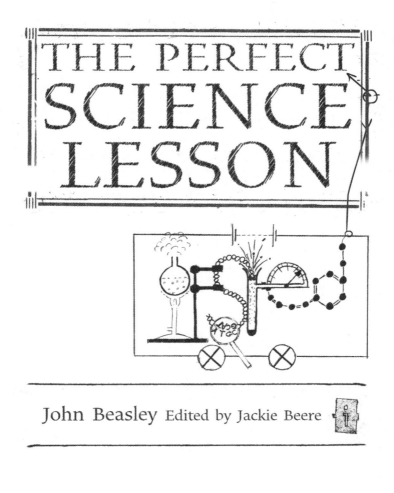

John Beasley Edited by Jackie Beere

Independent Thinking Press

First published by
Independent Thinking Press
Crown Buildings, Bancyfelin, Carmarthen, Wales, SA33 5ND, UK
www.independentthinkingpress.com

Independent Thinking Press is an imprint of Crown House Publishing Ltd.

British Library Cataloguing-in-Publication Data
A catalogue entry for this book is available
from the British Library.

Print ISBN 978-1-78135-130-7
Mobi ISBN 978-1-78135-190-1
ePub ISBN 978-1-78135-191-8
ePDF ISBN 978-1-78135-192-5

Printed and bound in the UK by
Gomer Press, Llandysul, Ceredigion

For the four women in my life: my wife Jackie and our three daughters Kirstie, Lucy and Carrie. Each in their own way has been a role model for all that is best in this book about how to approach learning, and life.

Contents

Acknowledgements

To all my teaching colleagues in the past, and to all those who still strive to make teaching more enjoyable and rewarding for all – especially my wife, Jackie. Thanks also to Crown House Publishing for all their help and support.

Foreword

As a child my favourite toy was my chemistry set. It seemed like magic to discover how heat, potions and powders created reactions that you couldn't always predict, and it made me feel powerful and grown up. Consequently, when I started secondary school, I loved science lessons and planned to work in a research lab, wearing a white coat and designing experiments that would change the world. That dream lasted well into my second year when science became separate subjects. My teachers did, indeed, wear white coats, but they started speaking a language that confused and frustrated me. The main activity seemed to be taking down copious notes and drawing Bunsen burners. During those years I lost my love of science and failed to connect it to my world.

Inspiring children through scientific exploration and connecting the science curriculum with the real world is an essential aspect of being an excellent science teacher. But sometimes the grind of exams, an overloaded curriculum and the pressure of Ofsted expectations can wear down even the most enthusiastic teacher. In this book science teachers can find practical ideas to use in their lessons and to establish the link between great teaching, professional development and Ofsted expectations. Great science teachers continually reflect on their practice, sustain rapport by getting feedback from pupils and, above all, sustain and develop a love of science in them by connecting science to the real world. Whatever stage you are at in your teaching career, it is vital to top up your vision and passion by reading some inspiring blogs or a book like this one.

The Perfect book series has delivered examples of good classroom practice linked to the latest research and to the feedback from various Ofsted reports and guidance. Often this guidance makes perfect sense, such as all subjects delivering on literacy, ensuring that learning is deep (not just for exams) or having no set structure for lessons.

The Perfect books also want to promote the idea that the quality of your teaching is dependent on your mindset and the habits you develop and model for the pupils. In this book, you can really see the connection between great teaching and great habits of learning, an ideal learning environment and relationships that enhance learning.

Whether you are new to teaching, in your early years as a teacher or are highly experienced, whether you are a primary or secondary teacher reflecting on your practice, this book will offer you the chance to stand back and consider what is working and how you can tweak your practice to improve and maybe even break unhelpful habits.

If you put a frog in a pan of boiling water it will immediately jump out and save itself. However, if you place it in a pan of cold water and very slowly bring the water to the boil the frog will die. Sometimes we don't notice when, gradually, we develop habits in our teaching that we aren't even aware of: the grumpy registration voice, tick and flick marking, asking the same pupils for answers or using dialect expressions that don't model standard English.

Then someone from Ofsted comes along and gives us feedback about our teaching that we don't recognise and we get angry because we think they are wrong. You can save yourself from this experience by taking the temperature of your teaching on a regular basis, as John suggests in this book. Self-awareness gives you the gift of immediate hindsight – you know your impact and you know what to do about it. As a scientist this will appeal to your own curiosity – and the very best teachers are endlessly curious about learning and how it works in their classroom.

My own science lessons delivered an exam result but eroded my curiosity about how things work. However, a fascination with how learning works is at the heart of great teaching. The changes in the examination framework mean science teachers have to find ways to help their pupils retain huge amounts of content through deeper learning and be able to transfer skills and understanding. To do this, the natural curiosity which is at the heart of science needs to be nurtured from the early years. The challenge for science teachers is to sustain and grow curiosity by modelling it. Some of the very best lessons I have ever observed have been science lessons that do exactly this.

Jackie Beere, Tiffield

Introduction

There is no 'perfect' lesson, not least because there are no perfect teachers or perfect pupils. However, that doesn't mean that we, and our pupils, shouldn't strive for perfection.

Ofsted have their version of this Holy Grail set out in the inspection framework and in the descriptors for outstanding in the inspection handbook. This book aims to give some practical advice to help science teachers along the road to perfection – or at least as far as outstanding. It describes the attributes of 'perfect' teachers and how, with a growth mind-set, you can work towards acquiring all of these. The book shows how you can develop great relationships with your pupils and how you can teach them the habits of effective learners, so that they can get closer to becoming 'perfect' pupils, and so become better scientists.

As Ofsted recently said:

'For pupils to achieve well in science, they must not only acquire the necessary knowledge, but also understand its value, enjoy the experience of working scientifically, and sustain their interest in learning it. Pupils in schools need to discover the concepts revealed through observing scientific phenomena and conducting experimental investigations for themselves. Then they are more likely to continue to study science and use that learning for work, for family, and to contribute as informed citizens.'

Ofsted (2013: 4)

Science teachers have the privilege of teaching a subject about which children are naturally curious. It is the subject that answers that great question 'Why?' and opens up pupils' minds to the wonders of both the microcosm and the macrocosm.

Chapter 1

Science Teaching: The State We're In

The intention of this opening chapter is to raise awareness of the issues faced by some primary and secondary schools (and the pupils in them). I describe pitfalls to avoid when teaching now and also when planning the introduction and teaching of the new science curriculum. There is a chance, finally, for good practical work (which pupils love) to become an integral part of learning about science, and for schools to develop a curriculum which truly values the subject and thereby produces model scientists. Let's take this chance and not repeat the mistakes of the past!

Even better if ...

Primary schools saw the end of statutory assessments in science in 2009 and, worryingly, the latest Trends in International Mathematics and Science Study (TIMSS) survey (Martin et al., 2012) showed that the performance of 10-year-olds in science had declined in English schools, relative to their previous survey in 2007. Concerns were also being voiced at this time by employers, higher education and professional scientific bodies that too many pupils were leaving secondary school with poor practical, investigative and analytical skills.

Against this background, Ofsted conducted a review of science teaching in both primary and secondary schools and published a report in 2013 entitled, *Maintaining Curiosity*. The report described the best way of raising achievement in science:

> 'The schools visited that made science interesting for their pupils, both primary and secondary schools, raised achievement in science. In both phases the most effective approach seen was through practically based investigations. Pupils experienced the scientific phenomena for themselves and then used that experience to raise their own further questions, thereby maintaining curiosity.'
>
> Ofsted (2013: 40)

The report celebrated good teaching practice and underlined how important practical work is to maintaining pupils' interest and future success in the subject. This is why practical work features so prominently later on in this book. Being an Ofsted report, it also described poor teaching practices. As you read on, consider whether or not you see any of these practices in your school, and also bear in mind that most (69%) of the science teaching seen was at least good!

There are indications, however, that some pupils are not always getting the best experience of this wonderful subject. I deal with concerns about the primary phase first, but as many of the issues raised are common to both phases, these should also be read by secondary teachers.

Poor primary (practical) practice

In the *Maintaining Curiosity* report, Ofsted noted this concern:

> 'Most teachers in the [primary] schools visited no longer provided pupils with time to revise and review their science knowledge, and most prioritised English and mathematics above science, which is still a core subject in the National Curriculum. This is a worsening of science provision since 2011, with about half of the school leaders in the report citing the removal of SATS as the main reason they no longer paid as much attention to science.'
>
> Ofsted (2013: 9)

Worrying enough, but some primary teachers and pupils actually saw science as a sort of respite from English lessons and as a subject where pupils didn't need to write much.

> 'At its worst, inspectors heard pupils say: "We like science because we do not have to write anything."'
>
> Ofsted (2013: 10)

They also found that:

> 'Almost half of the schools visited were not setting science targets. This emphasises starkly the decline of science, yet targets were set for English and mathematics because leaders and managers knew that this could bring about improvement in outcomes for pupils.'
>
> Ofsted (2013: 21)

Teaching English and maths at the expense of science is short-sighted because science can be an excellent vehicle for teaching these subjects *and* frees up curriculum time. So, use science to teach English and maths!

The main issues raised in the report, and some possible solutions, are set out in the table opposite.

Primary

What's wrong	How to put it right	Where to find this
Not enough time is given to revise and review pupils' science knowledge.	Spiral the curriculum to revisit and review previous work.	See Johnston (2012)
Almost half of the schools visited were not setting science targets.	Targets are known to improve outcomes for maths and English, so why not set targets for science?	See Chapter 2
Science has a lower priority than maths and English.	Use science as a vehicle for teaching literacy and numeracy (e.g. use science content as material for reading and writing non-fiction, use experimental data for graphical and other numeracy skills, make explicit connections between science and literacy). This practice shows clear evidence of better science and literacy outcomes for pupils (Ofsted, 2013: 10). When the same teacher teaches these subjects to the same pupils, and knows their strengths	

cont ...

Primary

What's wrong	How to put it right	Where to find this
	cont ... and weaknesses, why wouldn't they use science as a vehicle to do so if it improves outcomes and frees up time?	
The national curriculum content is not always fully covered and science is not being taught with enough emphasis on 'working scientifically'.	Plan for teachers to meet the overarching aims of the national curriculum for science. These aims spell out clearly the central role of scientific enquiry in developing pupils' ideas, skills, knowledge and understanding in a way that sustains their natural curiosity. Teach more of the content through a 'working scientifically' approach.	
Teachers do most of the planning of investigations for pupils, often with detailed step-by-step instructions on worksheets.	First, ascertain pupils' prior knowledge (of skills as well as content) before any practical work is carried out. Encourage more independent thinking especially among the most able. Allow pupils to propose their own	

	questions and then to plan, carry out and evaluate their own investigations in order to answer them.	
Pupils' skills of scientific enquiry are weak relative to learning content.	Teach these skills consistently year on year and allow the pupils sufficient time to develop them. Think first about control of variables or fair testing, then specifically develop pupils' skills of observation, drawing, measuring, recording, analysing and calculating. Teach them that designing and doing investigations is central, but that it is just as important to learn how to do this accurately, reliably and consistently. Use skills grids to do this.[1]	Show models and exemplars. See Chapter 2

---

1 See the grid produced by Nicky Waller of the National STEM Centre, which has been adapted for 'I can …' language in science at: http://www.tes.co.uk/ResourceDetail.aspx?storyCode=6407005.

Primary

What's wrong	How to put it right	Where to find this
Sometimes pupils are simply passive observers of practical work, with little opportunity to work independently.	Don't imagine that doing demonstration work is the same as doing practical work.	
It is essential that pupils develop a healthy scepticism about apparently 'scientific' facts.	Pupils need to recognise that established scientific knowledge is built on repeatable experimental observations and results, not one-off claims. Use stories from the media about the MMR vaccine, food scares, etc.	See note 2 below
Lesson planning is often not adequately differentiated.	Where this is done 'by outcome', make sure that there is sufficiently challenging material for the most able. Design effective, stepped proof activities.	See Chapter 2
Grouping by ability in science is rare.	Ability grouping is common for maths and English. Consider extending this into science.	

When pupils are paired by ability, it is the more able pupils who do most of the work.	Encourage individuals to perform proof activities after tasks.	See Chapter 2
The recording of progress is not as good as that for maths and English, and pupils in science know less about what they need to do to improve.	Identify and share success criteria and assess or get pupils to self-assess against these. Record the outcomes and then act on them.	See Chapter 2

2 See how Ben Goldacre's concept of 'bad science' is being used in the classroom at: http://www.badscience.net/ and http://www.collins. co.uk/page/Bad+Science. The latter website is aimed at Key Stage 3 and 4 but could be adapted for primary use.

Poor secondary (practical) practice

For both primary and secondary schools, the *Maintaining Curiosity* report found that:

> 'Science achievement in the schools visited was highest when individual pupils were involved in fully planning, carrying out and evaluating investigations that they had, in some part, suggested themselves.'
>
> Ofsted (2013: 6)

This is reinforced in the preamble to the Key Stage 3 national curriculum which says:

> 'Pupils should decide on the appropriate type of scientific enquiry to undertake to answer their own questions and develop a deeper understanding of factors to be taken into account when collecting, recording and processing data. They should evaluate their results and identify further questions arising from them.'
>
> Department for Education (2013: 3)

In the first years of secondary school, pupils *want* to pursue their own scientific interests and curiosity and often eagerly ask the question, 'Are we doing a practical today?' This is not surprising, considering most of their science lessons are

now taught in purpose-built laboratories and they are surrounded by the paraphernalia of practical science. They even
start off their secondary science careers learning all about
how to use this stuff safely. They are eager to do practical
work, and it is what they expected science to be about –
discovery through experiment!

But too many Year 7 pupils find themselves repeating practicals they did at primary school. They quickly find that the
curriculum straightjackets them into doing set practical work,
giving them little or no opportunity to pursue their own
scientific interests and curiosity. The opportunity for mean-
ingful practical work also decreases the older they get. For
many, the subject often turns into a dull succession of lessons
going through the textbook a double-page spread at a time,
copying down objectives, doing worksheets, learning yet
more 'stuff'. There is too little time to follow the pupils' interests and, by the end of Year 9, the by now plaintive cry of,
'Are we doing a practical today?' is heard less and less often.

In the Key Stage 4 science curriculum, what little practical
work pupils do in often-squeezed lesson time, is dominated
by controlled practical assessments. It can become a set of
formulaic procedures, akin to following a recipe, with the
outcomes known before the practical starts. It is done in
pairs or small groups, with many of the pupils only going
through the motions or even doing no practical work at all.
Too often, practicals become disconnected from content – a
content which, in turn, has often become disconnected from
pupils' lives.

According to Ofsted, in some secondary schools:

> 'Students sometimes had no voice in what they were being taught or any idea why the topic was being taught. As one student said, "I do not see how the practical activity is supposed to link to the science we are doing, and I cannot see what use that science has." At worst, students were told they would need it "for the exams". This does not secure students' interest, although it may tap into their concerns about their future success.'
>
> Ofsted (2013: 36)

In the quest for 'good' GCSE results, many schools understandably push the pupils hard and fast, meaning that there is not enough time to enrich and make the curriculum more relevant to pupils. But as Ofsted observed:

> 'Getting the grade is not the same as "getting" the science. Too frequently, GCSE grades indicated that students were doing well but they were not enjoying science.'
>
> Ofsted (2013: 26)

Counterproductively, and as a direct result of this experience, most students drop science post-16:

> 'Some sixth formers said they had not liked the lack of relevance of Key Stage 4 science and that this was why they did not choose physics – or, for some, any science – at 16.'
>
> Ofsted (2013: 26)

Even worse, and with even more short-sightedness:

> 'Most of the schools visited taught triple science in the same time allocation as double award science. This is too short a time if the courses do not start until Year 10: open-ended scientific enquiry and opportunities for independent learning are limited and students often find themselves attending after-school sessions to keep up. Although they attend, they do not want to repeat the approach in the sixth form, so motivation to study science in the future and take-up both decrease.'
>
> Ofsted (2013: 33)

This sort of pressure helps no one – including the teachers and their prospects of teaching post-16 science!

The report found that not enough science departments see take-up of science post-16 as a performance indicator, or even find out the reasons why pupils do (or do not) choose science in the sixth form. Neither do they track uptake in terms of ethnicity, pupil premium or gender or find out why there is a bias in some subjects. Getting feedback is crucial.

For the relatively few pupils who do choose to continue with science, the report goes on to say that they may have the GCSE grades, but not the science practical skills they need:

> 'Sixth-form teachers told inspectors that this lack of practical skill is revealed starkly for many students at A level, as they try to catch up with the demands of accurate, individual practical and experimental work.'
>
> Ofsted (2013: 33)

This is symptomatic of spending too little time on a limited range of practical work during GCSE.

There is a great deal of high quality teaching in sixth-form lessons (89% of lessons observed were good or better (Ofsted, 2013: 29)), but this was at odds with only adequate progress being found in just under half the schools, suggesting the pupils lack independent study skills when it comes to them becoming more responsible for their own learning.

The table below addresses some of the issues raised and suggests some ways to put them right:

Secondary

What's wrong	How to put it right	Where to find this
There is too little time to follow the pupils' interests.	Time *has* to be made for this in order to maintain interest and curiosity and allow the pupils opportunities to demonstrate the skills they have learned. Look hard at freeing up time by discarding or modifying 'recipe-based' practicals. Offer extra-curricular enrichment opportunities, such as a science activity week or STEM club.	See Chapter 2
Science curriculum time is often squeezed.	It is the job of science teams to persuade managers that a lack of time pressurises staff and pupils unfairly and that, even if achievement targets are reached, the evidence (e.g. Ofsted, 2013: 33) shows that uptake to and success in sixth-form courses are negatively impacted by it. *cont …*	See Chapter 2

Secondary

What's wrong	How to put it right	Where to find this
	cont ... Start GCSE courses in Year 9. Consider the impact of terminal examinations and the need for new ways to review and revise, such as 'flipped learning'.[3]	
GCSE practical work is dominated by controlled practical assessments. For many, other practical work has become a set of formulaic procedures.	Assuming the curriculum time is available, allow pupils to propose their own questions and then plan, carry out and evaluate their own investigations to answer them.	See Chapter 2
Practical work is done in pairs or small groups, with many of the pupils actually doing no practical work at all.	Routinely ask individuals to perform proof activities after tasks.	
Practicals have become disconnected from the content, which has become disconnected from pupils' lives.	Teach the content through practical work whenever possible, and try to connect learning to the real world of your pupils.	

Students have no voice in what they are taught or any idea why the topic is being taught.	Always make clear long-term aims and short-term objectives. Ensure pupils are involved in formulating their own success criteria.	See Chapter 2
Students are told they will need it 'for the exams'.	Never apologise for the content of any lesson. Turn it into a challenge.	
Not enough schools see take-up to science post-16 as a performance indicator.	Make sure this is surveyed in detail every year, including which careers or university courses sixth-form leavers take.	

Remember that the intention of this chapter has been to raise awareness of the pitfalls to avoid when teaching now and also when introducing and teaching the new science curriculum. It has also been aimed to show how important practical work is to maintaining the curiosity and enjoyment of pupils.

The rest of the book is devoted to strategies for developing this curiosity and helping you and your pupils to truly enjoy learning more about this wonderful subject.

3   For more on flipped learning visit: http://flippedlearning.org/.

Chapter 2

Outstanding Science Lessons

Every science lesson you teach should be exciting, encourage curiosity and teamwork, introduce new concepts and ideas, explain a little more about this wonderful subject and leave the pupils wanting more. Is this true for you? Do your pupils look forward to your lessons? Do they arrive at your classroom door keen to learn from the start? Do they eagerly ask, 'What are we learning today, Miss?'

This chapter includes some ideas for great lessons that you can try out tomorrow. However, Chapter 3 (on the prerequisites of outstanding science teaching) and Chapter 4 (on developing the dispositions essential for outstanding learning) will make these ideas work even more effectively, and will help you to get a resounding 'Yes!' to the questions above.

Be aware

Always be aware of your pupil audience – before any lesson as much as during it. Plan not only what you are going to do but also how you will explain the material in plain words, so that your pupils get a deep, clear knowledge and understanding of the ideas and concepts. Above all, be aware of, and keep taking, the learning temperature in the lesson. Don't tolerate off-task behaviours – quickly and consistently curb them.

Be aware that any observer in your lesson will not be focusing all their attention on you and what you are doing. Rather, their focus will be on what progress your pupils are making towards the aims of your lesson. Grow that useful extra pair of eyes in the back of your head, but always have one of them trained on yourself!

Remembering to find out what they already know

Be conscious of what prior knowledge the pupils may have of the lesson content and how it may link to previous work or other subject areas. If the pupils have very little or no knowledge of what you are talking about, they won't see a knowledge gap that is bridgeable but an 'unbridgeable knowledge chasm' (Hattie and Yates, 2014: 6). As a result, they will switch off learning the content because they have nothing to link it to.

When starting to discuss a new topic, also try to gauge pupils' general contextual knowledge. The more factual knowledge they already have in their background memory, the more they will find ways to tie this knowledge together – a process called chunking. This, in turn, frees up space in the working memory to allow in new ideas and content and relate this to what is already known. For a fascinating and clear discussion about these issues see Willingham (2009: Chapters 2 and 3).

Don't blind them with science

Never forget that you are an expert and thus 'Experts can become insensitive to how hard a task is for the beginner, an effect referred to as "the curse of knowledge"' (Hattie and Yates, 2014: 12). We all know of teachers who teach way above the level of their pupils. Always empathise with your pupils and try to see the learning through their eyes. Get down to their level and build up gradually from there.

Never assume anything! This applies not only to lesson content but also to pupils' learning strategies and practical skills. For example, if you are demonstrating how to set up apparatus, explain why they will be doing the practical and how it links to the content. Then set it up in small steps, visible to all. Allow the pupils to watch carefully, mentally rehearse the procedure and ask questions. Be especially careful to stress safety issues – you don't want to literally blind your pupils with science! For example, don't assume that they will know how to use a sharp knife properly, or when heating anything don't assume that they won't touch hot objects or that they will remember how you told them to use a Bunsen burner last week.

Knowing how to make the abstract concrete

Bearing in mind the points above, also be aware of the level of vocabulary that your pupils may have. A poor vocabulary will not only limit their understanding of what you say, but it will also limit their descriptive abilities and their capacity to connect different ideas and make sense of them.

Delivering literacy skills has always been important for science teachers, especially when helping pupils to become comfortable, even excited, about using scientific vocabulary. However, never assume that your pupils understand complex sentence construction and polysyllabic terminology. Listen to yourself. Try to speak at their level. If you do use complex key vocabulary, explain unfamiliar words carefully and use them in context often. Describe the origins and the construction of the words – for example:

- Atom: from the Greek *atomos*, meaning cannot be divided.
- Ammeter: from *ampere*, the unit of current, and *meter*, the Latin to measure.
- Mutation: from the Latin *mutationem*, a changing.
- Photosynthesis: from the Greek words *photo*, light and *synthesis*, making.[1]

---

1   For examples of biology root words visit: https://airport.unimelb.edu.au/ science/biolwords/ and for chemistry examples visit: http://www.csun.edu/ science/books/sourcebook/chapters/1-vocabulary/resources/chemistry_roots.pdf. Physics doesn't seem to have a list of root words but there is a complete list of all Greek and Latin roots at: http://en.wikipedia.org/wiki/List_of_Greek_ and_Latin_roots_in_English.

This is all part of every teacher delivering the essential communication skills in every lesson to support standard English and vocabulary development as outlined by Ofsted (2011).

As suggested above, always empathise with your pupils and try to see the learning through their eyes. Get down to their level and build up gradually, one step at a time, from there. When explaining difficult ideas and concepts, think of ways to physically or mentally model them, and connect the learning with ideas and knowledge the pupils already have. Engage their emotional brains by speaking as if you are telling a story and by using different intonation, pace, humour and passion. And constantly check that they are following you.

Here is an example of how you might introduce the concept of electrical current voltage and resistance to Key Stage 3 pupils.

First draw a very simple circuit (Diagram 1). Redraw it as a perspective diagram (as in Diagram 2). Ask the pupils to imagine zooming into the wire. What do they see? Atoms of a metal, like copper. Why is copper a conductor of electricity? Go on to describe the positive nuclei of the copper atoms as being surrounded by a cloud of negatively charged particles called electrons. The electrons act a bit like a cloud of flies buzzing around your head. Explain that some of the flies (electrons) are so far away that they are not very attracted to your head (nucleus). Now ask them to imagine that we have a lot of heads (copper nuclei) close together as if they were in a wire, like the heads of the pupils around this table ...

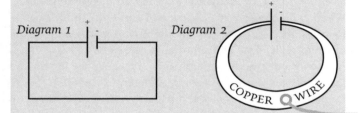

Approach the pupils and, using the end of your index finger to represent a fly (electron), show how it can randomly 'buzz' from atom to atom (head to head). Explain that lots of the electrons around copper atoms can move between copper atoms. It's a bit like the copper atoms in a wire are sitting in a cloud of electrons that can randomly buzz between and around different atoms. These electrons are 'free' (to move between different atoms). Stress that normally this movement is random so there is no overall flow of electrons in any particular direction in the wire (Diagram 3).

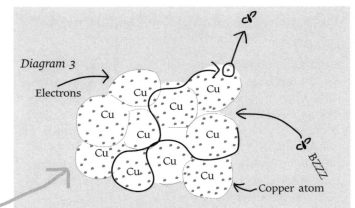

Diagram 3

Electrons

Cu Cu Cu Cu Cu Cu Cu Cu Cu

Copper atom

Now put a battery (technically a 'cell') into a circuit. Have the pupils ever noticed the plus and minus markings on a battery? Draw one, enlarged, on the board and pass around some batteries. Have they ever noticed that old batteries can leak nasty chemicals? Show an example (carefully) if you have one. These chemicals want to react together but need a supply of electrons to do so.

A battery will attract these negatively charged electrons in at the positive terminal (use 'unlike poles of a magnet' as an analogy for positive attracting negative). The chemicals in the battery use the electrons to help them react together and, afterwards, Violently (there's a reason for the capital V) push or throw them out of the other (negative) battery terminal. (*Don't* get into conventional and actual current today!) If all the chemicals in a battery react together, it stops working. The battery has 'run down' or 'lost its charge'.

Batteries left in a box don't run down because they can't get the electrons they need away from the gases in the air. (Atoms in gases hold onto their electrons too tightly. They are not 'free'.) But what happens if we put a loop of copper wire between the terminals as shown in Diagram 2? The positive battery terminal can now easily attract in some of the free electrons that are buzzing around the copper atoms, use them, and throw them out Violently at the negative terminal.

What happens when a battery pushes these negatively charged electrons out into the section of wire attached to the negative terminal? There are lots of negatively charged electrons already there.

What do like charges do? They repel each other (use 'like poles of a magnet' as an analogy). Pretend to be an electron! Tell a pupil that he is one too. Gradually approach him. What happens? Hopefully he moves away – he finds you repulsive!

Now you play the part of the battery, with a big plus sign on or over your right shoulder and a big minus sign over your left. Get all the pupils in the class to pretend to be electrons and get them to stand in a 'circuit' you have shown them which runs around the room. If the pupils bunch up around the circuit, remind them that they are electrons and find each other repulsive. Get them as a result to spread out evenly around your circuit (see Diagram 4).

One of the pupils will be unlucky enough to be nearest to your 'attractive', 'positive' right hand. Use it to pull the pupil (electron) in front of you and into the battery. Give the pupil a gentle shake as you use the pupil in your chemical reaction. Then push the pupil 'Violently' (actually gently!) out with your left hand. This pupil will bump into or get close to the pupil (electron) in the wire next to your negative terminal, who will be repelled and so will move away from the negative terminal. This repulsion is repeated all around the circuit, until you get a new victim who is forced to move next to your attractive positive terminal.

Repeat the process. Speed it up. What have we got? A flow of electrons. An electrical current.

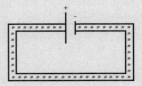

Diagram 4

Stop the current. Ask if anyone has heard of voltage or seen signs like 1.5V, 12V or 240V. Does anyone know what it means? It's equivalent to the Violence of the push or shoVe) of the battery. The more powerful the battery, the bigger the Voltage (shoVe) it can give to the electrons, and so the more energy it gives to each electron.

Now for resistance. How easy was it to get round the circuit? Was there anything stopping or resisting the pupils' movement? No? That's because the circuit had low resistance. The electrons found it easy to flow.

What if we put a gap in the circuit? What is in the gap? Answer: gases. (Not 'nothing'.) What did we learn about how easy it is for electrons to flow through gases? It is very hard for them. This is because gases have no free electrons which can flow between gas molecules. So gases have a big resistance – so big, in fact, that we normally refer to them as electrical insulators. Electrons find it very hard to flow through materials with no, or very few, free electrons. They would need a massive shoVe or Voltage to get them to jump across a gap in the circuit – much bigger than a normal battery can provide. But what would we see if they did jump? (A spark.)

What if we make the wire much narrower in one part of the circuit. This will restrict or resist the flow. The current will go down. What would happen to the current if we put a material in the circuit that doesn't have any or only has some free electrons?

Try out the ideas in the following diagrams using a pupil electron circuit:

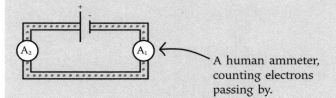

Current is the same all around a circuit. $A_1 = A_2$

Diagram 5a

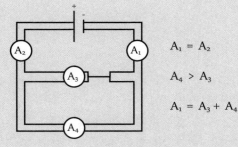

$A_1 = A_2$

$A_4 > A_3$

$A_1 = A_3 + A_4$

Diagram 5b

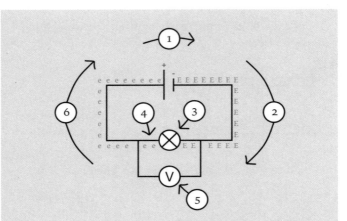

Diagram 5c

1. Cell pushes out electrons giving them energy E.

2. The electrons flow through the low resistance wire losing very little energy.

3. The bulb has a narrow high resistance wire (the filament). To get through the wire the electrons have to transfer energy to it, making it so hot it glows.

4. The electrons leave the bulb with less energy, e.

5. The voltage V is the difference between E and e.

6. The low energy electrons are pushed round back to the cell.

Always check they understand you

The most important thing of all to check is that the pupils understand. Every teacher knows that when explaining new content or describing instructions, you must constantly assess pupils' knowledge and understanding and act on the feedback. But do you check this regularly and *properly*?

Many teachers check for understanding by saying things like, 'Do you understand?' or 'Is everyone OK?' in the vague direction of the class. They forget that pupils who don't understand are not very likely to say so.

There are lots of strategies for checking understanding in 'Monitoring strategies or plenaries?' later in this chapter.

Starting the science lesson journey

If you can engage the pupils at the start, and then maintain this engagement, you are more than halfway there to an outstanding lesson. But your pupils must settle quickly and get on with the lesson without huge effort from you. This means that they need to know your expectations and how to efficiently and effectively carry out routine tasks.

Having routines

Routines show pupils that you are organised and have high standards and high expectations. If you set out clearly what these routines are, and consistently apply them, you will quickly get your pupils' respect. If you are an experienced teacher, check that your routines are working for you. If not, change them until they are. Routines become habits that show the 'typical' culture in your classroom.

So, as early as possible get your pupils familiar with:

- Seating plans. ☑
- Orderly yet speedy entry to the classroom or lab. ☑
- Your expectations for their learning behaviours – for example: ☑
  - When you speak, they listen and have their eyes on you.
  - How you expect the pupils to work as a team and give unconditional support to each other.
  - The habits of great learners.
- Your expectations of work standards (e.g. have exemplars ready to show the pupils). ☑
- Their responsibilities (e.g. homework, what to bring to lessons) and stress that you expect the pupils to remind each other of these. ☑
- How to ask questions. ☑
- Where to put their bags so that you can circulate freely around the room and own it. ☑
- Where apparatus and other materials are stored. ☑
- Health and safety in practical work – for example: ☑
  - Use of goggles or safety clothing.
  - Safe use of apparatus.

- Disposal of waste materials.
- How to safely react if they hear command words, like 'Stop!' in practical or other work.
- How to clear up and put things away properly after practical work.

▨ Lesson routines, such as what to do if they see ☑
starter activities or lesson objectives on the board.

Get the pupils to practise these routines and, where necessary, show them how to do it initially. Get them to work as a team to complete tasks. Tell them how good other classes are at these tasks and how long they take to do them. Remind them how long it took them to do a task last time. This takes up time at first, but it will be worth it in the long run.

Above all, be consistent in applying your routines and expectations in every lesson! Use sanctions fairly and consistently, if necessary. Constantly communicate your love of, and enthusiasm for, science, how you will help them to learn about science and your unflinching belief that they will. Convince them that every lesson you teach is an important step in their learning journey. In this way, they will learn to respect, like and maybe even love you and your subject. (See also 'What makes an outstanding science teacher?' in Chapter 3).

Getting them curious: inspiring mystery and wonder

What pupils experience in the first couple of minutes of a lesson is crucial to how well they engage with you and your learning intentions, and how they will progress towards knowing and understanding the lesson.

So, having banged on about the importance of routines, avoid routine *starts* to your lessons. There is nothing more boring than having the same activity at the beginning of every lesson – especially if it's simply copying down the objectives or listening to you for ages!

> 'The most common weakness was teachers talking too much at the start of a lesson.'
>
> Ofsted (2013: 15)

Being unpredictable at the start of every lesson makes your pupils wonder, before they ever get to your classroom, how the next lesson will start. They will look forward to finding out – and so be engaged before the lesson begins.

'Physicians take an oath that commits them to "first do no harm". The best science teachers, seen as part of this survey, set out to "first maintain curiosity" in their pupils. The most successful schools visited during this survey had adopted this as a key principle in teaching science and this not only fostered enthusiasm for the subject in their pupils but helped them to fulfil their potential.'

Ofsted (2013: 4)

Mysterious science starters

For all of the different types of curiosity-raising starters below, if there are questions to answer, insist on written responses from pupils working individually, in pairs or in groups. This shows the pupils that you value the exercise, and it gives you a means of gauging participation and understanding:

- Set up demonstration apparatus for the lesson where everyone can see it. Display one or more questions about what this might be for, how it relates to the last lesson, what the names of the components are, what energy transfers there might be or any other related questions.

- Do the same but hide the apparatus under a cloth. Before revealing it, ask questions about what it might be. Be really hammy about the mystery and the reveal!

■ Put out apparatus, objects, specimens, photos and the like on desks or around the room.

■ Pass around mystery objects related to the lesson in sealed bags and get the pupils to guess the contents, their purpose and so on.

■ Hand out or have ready the materials and instructions for a task (e.g. constructing a circuit, assembling apparatus) as soon as the pupils arrive in the classroom. Get them to work out what they are doing and why.

■ Greet them wearing a lab coat, rubber boots, protective gloves and visor or goggles!

■ Give the pupils the instructions for a practical activity cut up into strips inside an envelope. The first task is for them to work in groups to sort the instructions into a logical order.

■ Show a short video running on a loop (it's even better still if you have filmed it and star in it, perhaps with some pupils). Prepare and hand out some questions about the content.

■ Fill the room with (safe) smells.

■ Record a short story, explanation of a concept or instructions to do a task and play it when the pupils arrive. Prepare a written exercise to go with it.

■ Play a short video that you or a pupil made during the last lesson to recap work.

■ When they arrive, get some of the pupils to pick a number from a box. The numbers correspond to pupils' names and denote who will answer questions later.

■ Write a question or statement on the board, such as 'Is global warming happening?' or 'Nuclear energy is clean', and indicate an imaginary line down the side of the room. At one end is 'Agree' and at the other is 'Disagree'. As the pupils arrive, they should choose where they will stand along the line and think of reasons to justify their position.

■ Display some data or a graph on the board and ask the pupils to look for patterns.

■ Display a puzzling picture and an associated question.

■ Tell the pupils a story or anecdote, especially if it involves you (pupils love to find out more about their teachers). Be dramatic and engaging.

■ Organise for a visitor to be standing in the room.

If you want to recap work from the last lesson, try these techniques:

■ Display true/false statements or questions with short/one-word answers. As you ask a question, each pupil writes the answer on a mini whiteboard so the others cannot see. Then ask to them to 'show me'.

■ Ask a pupil to stand and talk for one minute about the topic that was covered in the last lesson/homework. At the first repetition, pause or mistake, another randomly chosen (or volunteer) student takes over. This works better if the class know in advance that they will be asked to do this.

■ Get a pupil or pair of pupils to act as the teacher and summarise what was covered in the last lesson/homework. They should also prepare quick questions to ask the class about what was studied. Go down the register so everyone gets a turn to do this and time to prepare.

■ Ask the pupils to deliver a short presentation that they have prepared at home. It could be to recap the last lesson's work or to introduce this lesson.

You could also try out the mood for learning exercise in Chapter 4 which can get lessons off to a good start – even on a depressing, wet Wednesday afternoon!

Whatever you try, think outside of the box to create starters which engage, enthuse, remind and provide variety. Try to involve the pupils whenever you can – you don't want them listening to your voice for too long without a question/answer or other input from them.

Starting the lesson with a bang

As a science teacher you can do this literally! Alternatively, start the lesson with a fascinating demonstration that has impact – for example, the collapsing aluminium can.[2] Obviously, it makes sense to tie these starters to the main body of the lesson, but sometimes there is nothing wrong with doing a demonstration to recap past work or just for the sheer fun of it. (But perhaps not when an inspector calls!)

---

2   See this in action at: http://www.youtube.com/watch?v=FjYB8hgkvOU.

Follow the demo with a quick-fire question-and-answer session during which the pupils try to explain what they have seen. As key words emerge from the discussion, ask one pupil to write them on the board. Then get the class to use these to produce an account explaining the science behind what they have seen.

A suggestion made by Daniel Willingham is to consider 'whether these strategies might be used not only at the beginning of a lesson but also *after* the basic concepts have been learned' (Willingham, 2009: 21). He fears that pupils might regard demonstrations as being like a magic trick, and therefore they might not engage in a sustained way to understand the principles behind them.

To avoid this problem, you could present the collapsing can at the beginning of a lesson, for example, and then have another related demonstration (like the egg in a bottle[3]) at the end of the lesson or at the start of the next lesson. Use this to reinforce and drive home the scientific principles at work.

Finishing the starter

No matter what type of starter you choose to do, always make it pacy and don't let it go on for too long – far too many do. When you finish, link what the pupils have just seen, heard or done to the main body of the lesson and tell

---

3   Burn a piece of paper in a milk bottle. When the flames die down, immediately put a moist soft-boiled egg on top. The egg is pushed into the bottle.

them how great the content is going to be, how they will become experts in it, what they will learn from it and what they will be able to do as a result. Be upbeat and energised. Your mood should be infectious and spread to the pupils. Sometimes, at the end of a long, hard term, you may have to fake the energy and enthusiasm for Year 8 on a Friday afternoon, but if you do you will enjoy it more – and so will they!

Having said all that about starter activities, if the lesson plan does not include one because you are continuing a topic from last time, then fine. Get the pupils settled quickly and on task. Alternatively, you may have received feedback from your last lesson that all did not go well. The starter can be used to put this right – hopefully in an engaging way.

There is a searchable database of starters, including short videos and masses of other useful materials, all of which can be downloaded from the National STEM Centre's website.[4]

---

4   Visit: http://www.nationalstemcentre.org.uk/. You will need to register (for free) to make the best use of this.

Mapping the route

'Lessons that teachers set into a bigger "learning journey" allowed pupils to see how the element of learning in the lesson connected to the bigger scheme of things. That led to learning intentions that lasted for several lessons, for example work on dissolving solids in liquids was a step towards evidence for the particulate nature of matter. At the highest level the most effective teachers constructed lessons that connected explicitly with other subject areas, notably English and mathematics. This allowed pupils to relate learning across subjects, and to use science as the context for others.'

Ofsted (2013: 41)

Clear lesson aims and objectives

Whatever starter you choose, you will usually have to follow it with an explanation of what the rest of the lesson will be about and how it fits in with the overall aim. The aim (or learning outcome) of a lesson gives a broad idea of what you hope pupils will have achieved by the end of the lesson (or sequence of lessons). It explains what the lesson objectives are leading towards. A goal is simply a more precise way of writing an aim.[5]

When planning a lesson, always start with the overall aim and plan backwards from it. Break the aim down into discrete lesson objectives, or learning targets, which are short statements about the measurable steps the pupils need to take to achieve the aim. They should show what the pupils will be able to do as a result of their learning in the lesson. They should be testable in order to evidence progress towards the overall aim. Objectives or learning targets should also help to give the pupils a context for the learning – a reason for doing the lesson. These need to be on show and referred to throughout the lesson.

Learning targets are usually expressed as an 'I can ...' statement, which clearly communicates what the pupils will be able to do at the end of the lesson and/or the learning. For example, 'I can explain to [my parents] how haemophilia is inherited' or 'I can use a dichotomous tree to classify invertebrates'. There is an excellent discussion of these and other great lesson strategies in Berger et al. (2014: 31). Highly recommended!

Check that the objectives or targets are:

- Short and in clear, pupil-friendly language (but don't forget to unpick any complex terms that have to be there). ✓

- Challenging yet achievable. ✓
- Progress the pupils stepwise towards the overall aim. ✓
- As far as possible, worthwhile, real, relevant and important to the pupils (i.e. connected to their lives).[6] ✓
- SMART (specific, measurable, achievable, realistic and time-related). ✓
- Thought of as motivational (i.e. achievement of them is a time to celebrate success!). ✓

It is crucial that objectives are measurable in some way. How else are the pupils going to know they have achieved the objectives? So, make sure that you and the pupils:

- Can easily assess the objectives using some sort of proof activity. ✓
- Can describe the success criteria for each one. ✓

The last point is very important and will be addressed in more detail later in this chapter. But first, because there is so much content in science, objectives very often start with, 'Pupils will know …'. For example, 'Pupils will know that exothermic chemical reactions release energy' or 'Pupils will know the path of electrical impulses in a simple reflex arc'. These are fine so long as they describe what the pupils will be learning and can be *easily* measured. Also useful in practical work are 'Be able to …' objectives, such as, 'Pupils will be able to heat

---

6 For example, instead of writing a target in terms of, 'I can describe how a detergent works', try to put this into a familiar context such as, 'I can describe how detergents get my friend's greasy hair clean'.

safely using a Bunsen burner' or 'Pupils will be able to use a measuring cylinder to accurately measure volume'.

Try to use a range of verbs in objectives like analyse, compare, contrast, create, define, demonstrate, describe, discuss, explain, identify and so on. For the really keen, the Center for Teaching and Learning at the University of North Carolina at Charlotte has produced a good summary of the methods for writing objectives based on Bloom's Taxonomy,[7] and Appendix 5 has a full list of verbs related to the different cognitive levels in the Taxonomy. Beware of objectives like, 'Pupils will understand the causes of global warming' or 'Pupils will learn about how digestion works', because they are not easily measurable without extensive questioning or testing. These would make better aims rather than objectives.

Finally, put yourself in the pupils' shoes and ask yourself what they would have to do to show they really understand the aims, objectives or targets. This will get you thinking about success criteria and about what sort of proof activities best show progress. Better still, get the pupils to devise the success criteria with you (there is more on this later in this chapter).

---

7 See: http://teaching.uncc.edu/learning-resources/articles-books/best-practice/
   goals-objectives/writing-objectives.

Chapter 2

Challenge

Always consider the following questions when thinking about aims, objectives or targets:

■ Are they at the right level, or are they too easy/too hard?

■ Have the pupils got the prior knowledge, strategies and skills needed to achieve them?

■ Am I looking at the level of challenge through the pupils' eyes?

Some teachers, conscious of their mixed ability classes, split objectives into, 'All will ...', 'Most will ...' and 'Some will ...'. For example, in a lesson with the aim, 'To understand what an electric current is', the objectives were:

■ *All* will know that a complete circuit is required for an electric current to flow.

■ *Most* will know that current is a flow of electrons.

■ *Some* will know that a potential difference is required for an electric current to flow.

The thinking is that that this will allow differentiation. Unfortunately, this can be seen by some pupils as a ticket to do only the work which requires the least possible effort. Some bright, fixed mindset pupils may see addressing only the easier objectives as a means of avoiding failure. And some lower ability pupils may see these as the teacher putting a ceiling on their expectations.

Also, to fully meet the lesson aim, all three objectives/statements need to be understood. Why not simply drop the 'all', 'most' and 'some' and challenge *all* the pupils to go for *all* the objectives? You could think of the first objective as being the minimum that you want the pupils to learn, therefore your lesson plan must include an activity which allows it to be demonstrated. But to evidence progress, your lesson plan will also need a proof activity which assesses or tests whether or not the pupils have met this objective. It is this proof activity that can be differentiated. This process should then be repeated for each of the objectives.

If you feel that you must get the pupils to write down the learning objectives, insist that they only have one minute to do it. There are lots of ways to go about it:

- Jumble up the words.
- Cut and paste them.
- Leave words missing from them for the students to fill in.
- Write up key words and get the pupils to write down the objective(s).
- Ask pupils to leave a space in their books and do this at the end of the lesson.

Going SOLO

SOLO (Structure of the Observed Learning Outcome), developed by Biggs and Collis (1982), provides another

48

approach to setting objectives based on different levels of understanding:

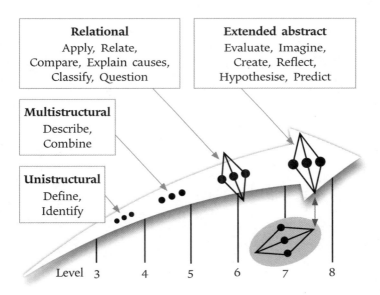

Source: Adapted from Biggs and Collis (1982).

Let's use SOLO to see how ideas about photosynthesis might develop:

Level			Photosynthesis example	SOLO verbs[8]
Prestructural No ideas			Pupils start with little or no knowledge of the topic. They may have a general knowledge that plants are green and need light and water to survive, but not much else.	**Seeking clarification** 'I'm not sure why ...' 'I'm confused because ...' 'Where should I begin to ...' 'I suppose I could ...'
Unistructural An idea	**Unistructural** Define, Identify	●→ ●●	Pupils know (securely) one thing, such as, 'Plants take in carbon dioxide as part of the photosynthetic process'.	**Getting started** 'To begin with ...' 'Amazingly ...' 'I'll start with ...' 'We found that ...'
Multistructural Many ideas	**Multistructural** Describe, Combine	●→ ●●	Pupils know more than one thing about the topic. For example, the fact above, plus, 'Plants take in water through their roots and capture light energy using the green chlorophyll in their leaves'	**Adding** 'As well ...' 'Plus ...' 'Also ...' **Combining** 'Together ...'

Relational **Relating ideas**	**Relational** Apply, Relate, Compare, Explain causes, Classify, Question 	Pupils can relate their multistructural knowledge and demonstrate how this links together. For example, pupils can take their knowledge of photosynthesis and create a word, chemical equation or annotated diagram to demonstrate how photosynthesis works.	'Combined ...' **Evidence** 'This is shown by ...' 'We know because ...'
		and 'Plants also produce glucose and oxygen in the process'.	**Cause** 'This is due to ...' **Effect** 'Due to this ...' **Similarity** 'In the same way ...' **Contrast** 'Alternatively ...' **Sequencing** 'First ...' 'Next ...'

For more on SOLO verbs visit: http://pic.twitter.com/duoeqTQgm and for more on SOLO in general visit: http://pamhook.com/free-resources/downloadable-resources/.

Level		Photosynthesis example	SOLO verbs
Extended abstract Extending ideas	**Extended abstract** Evaluate, Imagine, Create, Reflect, Hypothesise, Predict	Pupils can take their learning on photosynthesis and apply it to other scenarios, e.g.: 'If this happens with plants, what happens with algae?', 'Variegated plants may be ...', 'What about levels of CO_2 in the atmosphere ...?', 'I can teach others about photosynthesis'.	**Commenting** 'The most important thing is ...' 'In my opinion ...' **Concluding** 'In conclusion ...' 'To summarise ...' **Anomalies/Exceptions** 'Very occasionally ...' 'An exception is ...' **Forecasting/Predicting** 'If this continues then ...' **Hypothesising** 'I'm led to propose that ...'

Source: Adapted from Anderson (2013: 37).

A very good example of SOLO is found in Hattie (2012: 61). In this example, a science teacher used either a verbal or written quiz to find out what his pupils knew about this learning objective: 'Recognise that light and sound are types of energy detected by ears and eyes'. Once he knew their starting points, he asked his pupils to work through a grid like this one (after supplying them with key words and equipment):

Level	Learning intention	Success criteria
Uni/ Multistructural	Recognise that light and sound are forms of energy and have properties.	I can name one or more properties of light and sound.
Relational	Know that light and sound can be transformed into other types of energy.	I can explain how light and sound are transformed into other types of energy.
Extended abstract	Understand how light and sound allow us to communicate.	I can discuss how light and sound help us to communicate.

This gives the pupils some well-defined success criteria to aim for and shows them how complex each criterion is. It also gives the teacher a clear idea of how well each pupil has progressed from their starting point (providing that there is one or more proof activity for each criterion).

But to really help pupils achieve the necessary criteria and progress, we also need to include the following elements in our lessons.

Modelling and sharing the success criteria

Start with the end in mind. If one of your objectives is to get the pupils to draw a diagram of some apparatus show them a WAGOLL (What A Good One Looks Like). Show them exemplary models of everything – completed graphs, use of apparatus, experimental write-ups and so on. Describe their strengths and possible weaknesses. Show the pupils exactly what you are looking for.

Go from the simple to the complex. For example, for results tables:

- This was drawn with a sharp pencil and ruler.
- The lines in the table are parallel to each other.
- The headings are clear, including units.
- The independent variable goes in the first column.
- The different measurements of the independent variable are set out like this ...

▓ The mean or average value is calculated like this … and shown in this column.

▓ This mean current has been calculated correctly as 9.56 amps, but is it right to show two numbers after the decimal point?

When Ron Berger was an apprentice carpenter, the master carpenter showed him examples or models of what to do. He says of this: 'No amount of words could convey what one good model taught me. I carried around that vision in my head and I always knew what I was striving for: I had a picture of what quality looked like' (Berger, 2003: 83).

He goes on: 'I want my students to carry around pictures in their head of quality work. It's not enough to make a list, a rubric, of what makes a good essay or a good science experiment. This is an important step, but it doesn't leave a picture, a vision, an inspiration. It's not even enough to read a great piece of literature together and analyse the writing, or to look at the work of a great scientist.'

Using critique to discover WAGOLL

If Berger wants his pupils to write a great essay or write up an experiment, he shows them what a great essay or experiment write-up looks like. He then works together with his pupils on these models to critique them, to admire their strengths and to find weaknesses in them. Use models so that your pupils can find inspiration in the work of others and use it to better themselves.

For example, a critique session could be used to get your pupils to write up scientific methods properly:

- Give out enlarged (laminated) photocopies of a pupil's work. (Make sure it is an excellent write-up with which you are very familiar.) Seeing this immediately makes the exercise more real for your pupils.

- Tell the class that there are always three basic rules to follow when discussing or critiquing someone else's work: be kind, be specific, and be helpful.[9] Write these on the board.

- Get the pupils to read out sections of the write-up to the rest of class and then discuss it among themselves to discover what makes it a quality piece of work.

- Get them to use dry-wipe pens to highlight or annotate the laminated piece to show evidence of quality in the work.

- Question the class and harvest their ideas, asking them to read aloud the parts of the write-up they think show these qualities.

- Note the ideas on the board, perhaps rephrasing them for clarity, e.g. 'Clear structure', 'Underlined headings', 'Complete apparatus list', 'Logical method, easy to follow'.

- If they miss important points pose questions like, 'Did the writer spell all the scientific words correctly?' 'Was the work legible?' 'Did the writer control all the variables?' Add these to the list on the board.

---

9 See Berger (2003: 92–96) for details on these and other guidelines used in critique sessions.

■ By the end of this process, the pupils themselves will have discovered the success criteria for an excellent write-up.

A critique session also teaches the pupils to think metacognitively about their own work, so that when they do their own write-up they are better able to self-assess it, or peer assess someone else's work if asked to do so.

Modelling modelling

Berger has spent his life building up a library of good work from his own and from other schools. He has a range of models: photographs and photocopies of project work and posters, actual models pupils have made and videos of pupil presentations. He has sets of early drafts and redrafts of work he can show pupils, so they can see how to improve their work. He also has model pupil self-assessments which pupils can discuss and learn from.

Get your school or department to build up a similar library of model work. Have model work pinned up in your room, stored electronically or have several copies of, for example, excellent graphs put into prominently placed WAGOLL folders for the pupils to refer to. Use these for your critique sessions. Create rubrics for drawing graphs, writing up an experiment and so forth on take-away worksheets (but kept in a separate folder that only comes out *after* a critique session).

When you've had a critique session with your pupils, decided on the success criteria and then, possibly, distributed a rubric, tell them that this constitutes your expectation of the standard for their work. No excuses! If they turn in below par material, feed this back to them and get them to redraft it. (There is more on assessment and feedback below.)

Top tips

Ensure that the following apply to the success criteria you use:

- They are clear and achievable (at least to some degree) by everyone in the class. ☑
- The pupils have some input into designing them and so have some ownership of them. ☑
- They matter to the pupils (i.e. they can see the benefits of achieving them). ☑
- You've helped the pupils to use their imaginations to see, feel or otherwise experience what success would be like. ☑
- They are testable. Given this, what proof activities will you use to evidence progress? ☑

Finally, think carefully about whether there is or isn't any benefit in you levelling or grading the success criteria. Will doing this only benefit the more able?

Engaging tasks

How you plan for the pupils to achieve your objectives is up to you. There is no right or wrong way to do so. It is also acceptable for there to be lots of teacher talk:

'For example, [inspectors] should not criticise teacher talk for being overlong or bemoan a lack of opportunity for different activities in lessons unless there is unequivocal evidence that this is slowing learning over time. It is unrealistic, too, for inspectors to expect that all work in all lessons will be matched to the specific needs of each individual pupil. Inspectors should not expect to see pupils working on their own or in groups for periods of time in all lessons. They should not make the assumption that a particular way of working is always necessary or desirable. Its effectiveness depends on the impact of the quality and challenge of the work set. Pupils may rightly be expected to sit and listen to teachers, which of itself is an 'active' method through which knowledge and understanding can be acquired effectively. Inspectors should not criticise 'passivity' as a matter of course and certainly not unless it is evidently stopping pupils from learning new knowledge or gaining skills and understanding.'

Ofsted (2014b: 57–58)

This means that almost the entire lesson could be spent with the pupils doing nothing but listening to and watching you. This is fine – Ofsted say so! – providing that the lesson lends itself to this approach, that you have a captivating way of explaining the material, that strategies are in place to show progress and that you have vast amounts of energy to keep this up. Not everyone could do this lesson after lesson, so we need other strategies which put more onus on the pupils, yet are engaging – lessons like those with the 7C's.

The 7C's

If you are charting a leaning journey you might want it to include the 7C's: *challenge, criteria, collaboration, communication, creativity, competition* and *choice*. Planning these elements into your lessons helps to encourage many of the habits we want to foster in outstanding learners and helps lessons to become more enjoyable for all.

1. *Challenge*. Believe it or not, nearly all pupils enjoy a challenge, providing they don't see it as being too hard or too easy. Always pitch the challenge towards the upper end of what you think your pupils are capable of – and see how many times they surprise you!

2. *Criteria*. The pupils need to know what a good one looks like (WAGOLL) and what the success criteria

are. If you can get the pupils to help decide these, they will be better engaged with the task. After all, they have helped to set the bar.

3. *Collaboration*. When designing tasks, try to get pupils to work collaboratively with one another and share out different aspects of a challenge between members of a team. This is not something that comes naturally to everyone. As Zoë Elder (2012: 25) points out, pupils often need to know not only *how* to learn collaboratively but also *why* they are doing so. She gives lots of great advice about setting up effective collaborative learning.

4. *Communication*. Pupils will certainly be practising their communication skills in order to work collaboratively and in discussions with one another about whether the team is meeting the success criteria. Of course, these skills can also be shown in their written work and in presentations to the class.

5. *Creativity*. Get the pupils to use skills not often found in most run-of-the-mill lessons. Get them drawing, acting, presenting, designing, building or otherwise doing. You will find talents which otherwise would have remained hidden!

6. *Competition*. An element of competition in activities tends to get the adrenaline going and keep pupils focused on tasks for longer. This is especially true if

they are working in teams, as individual pupils don't want to be seen as letting the side down.

7. *Choice.* Involve pupils in co-designing the learning – for example, getting them to help decide how you and they might sequence lessons in a topic or determine success criteria for lessons. It could also come from trying an activity like the choice sheets explained later in this chapter.

Focus your planning using the 7C's. Whenever possible, try to include most or all of these elements in your plan, whatever the main task is in your lesson.

Marketplace activities

Marketplace activities are excellent for getting the pupils to become much more involved in the lesson and in an enjoyable way. The idea is that the pupils teach and learn from each other and so do the majority of the work. Most importantly, they make it easy for you, the pupils themselves or any observer present to see progress towards the lesson's aims and objectives.

The following example shows how this strategy can be used to teach the effects of global warming.

Chapter 2

The global warming marketplace activity

For this task, split the class into nine or ten groups of three.

You will need:

- ▨ Two or three sheets of A3 paper per group.
- ▨ Two or three large felt-tip pens per group.
- ▨ A few large sticky note sheets per group.
- ▨ Two reporter's notepads per group (these can be sheets of plain A5 paper stapled together).
- ▨ Five (or more if you wish) laminated sheets full of densely typed facts and figures about a different possible effect of global warming. Each sheet must contain a date when this effect is likely to kick in.
- ▨ Another laminated copy of each sheet (making ten in all).
- ▨ A stopwatch or a countdown timer on the board.

The hardest part of setting up marketplace activities is preparing the information sheets. However, in many cases you can simply copy and paste online newspaper articles or other online material like passages from books, or even laminate photocopies of textbooks (providing that there are no copyright issues). You can also add to or edit the text if you wish. You don't have to worry too much if the material looks dense and uninviting – part of the challenge is for the pupils to glean the important facts from the sheets.

Begin by making the task appear to be very challenging. Say something like:

You will learn about the effects of global warming, the order that they are likely to happen in, make posters about this and teach the details of these effects to each other – all in the next 30 minutes!

Show the class one of the daunting-looking sheets of information and then display slides showing the following rubric (or similar):[10]

1. You will be working in groups of three. (*You might want to choose the groupings.*[11])

2. Each group will be given one of five different data sheets about a possible effect of global warming. (*Hand out the ten laminated sheets, one to each group, face down.*)

3. Each group will elect one person, the 'teacher', to stay at base camp to teach the others about your effect. The other two will be 'reporters' sent out to find out about the other four effects. Elect the 'teacher' now. (*Once this is done, tell the pupils to turn over their information sheets.*)

4. Read and absorb the information on your sheet about the effect you have been given. **You have three minutes to do this.** (*Start a timer.*)

---

10   Note: the text in brackets is to help you (the teacher).
11   If the task requires mathematical or other specialist skills, you might want to put less able pupils with the more able.

5. Each group now has to create a visual aid on the A3 paper about their effect. The visual aid can have **only six words**, but it can have as many pictures, diagrams, symbols and numbers in it as you like. (*Discuss the WAGOLL/success criteria for the posters.*) **You have three minutes to do this.** (*Start a timer and circulate. After three minutes, instruct the pupils to turn the laminated cards face down.*)

6. Now send out the 'reporters' to find out about and take notes on the other four effects. **You have three minutes to do this by listening to the other 'teachers' explain their visual aid.** (*Start a timer.*)

7. Reporters now return and teach your team about all the other effects. **You have 3 minutes to do this.** (*Start a timer.*)

8. Each group now has to make a table with the names of the effects and the order in which they will happen and write this down on a sticky note. **You have one minute to do this.** (*Start a timer.*)

9. To finish, make up a name or draw a symbol to represent your group and add this to your sticky note. (*Ask the pupils to put the finished, and now identifiable, sticky notes on the wall.*)

With great drama and ceremony, display a PowerPoint slide to reveal the answers, one at a time, in the correct order.

Reward the winning teams with prizes. You could also have other prizes for the most imaginative posters.

To consolidate the knowledge, have the class note down the correct sequence of the effects, and then ask the 'teachers' with the best posters to explain them to the rest of the class, who take notes. You could also put up the best posters in sequence on the wall.

Marketplace activities are effective because they use peer learning and they contain six out of the 7C's. The one that is missing is choice, which can be remedied using ...

Flipped learning

Take a science topic and split it into ten or so different aspects in each of which the pupils have to learn some ideas, content and/or meanings of words. Give one aspect to a group of three pupils and set them a homework in which they independently learn or research this aspect. In the next lesson, give each group 15–20 minutes to pool their research and create a visual aid summary. They then use this in a marketplace activity where they and all the other groups teach and learn from each another.

This helps the pupils to learn more content in an engaging way and deepen that learning by doing a classroom activity with it.

Chapter 2

Choice sheets

These provide pupils with at least some element of choice of activity in a lesson. Even if you leave the pupils no choice but to do them all, at least they will be able to choose the order they do them in.

An example, adapted from the Year 5 Earth and Space programme of study, is shown in Appendix 3, but the same method of production could be used for any other topic.[12]

You could first introduce the topic with engaging starters such as videos[13] or a discussion about their prior knowledge. You might then:

- Ask the pupils to look at each task in turn and discuss their relative difficulty.
- Decide what the success criteria would be for each task.
- Assign a number of points for each task, depending on its difficulty.
- Organise the pupils into groups to complete each of the tasks on the sheet.

---

12 The worksheet in Appendix 3 was produced simply by cutting and pasting the programme of study into a Word document, and then arranging the text into speech bubbles (changing the wording as necessary). As you will note, not all the practical work suggested in the non-statutory guidance is included. This, along with other activities, could be put into another worksheet.

13 For a musical introduction with lots of solar system terminology to note down and discuss see: https://www.youtube.com/watch?v=h1mYYND8M_o, or this video shows the relative size of the planets and stars: https://www.youtube.com/watch?v=CubFmoRvwWQ.

- Award points against the success criteria when they have finished, either by self-assessment, by peer assessment or by you.
- An element of competition could also be introduced – if the points mean prizes!

Another version, on the circulatory system, aimed at sixth formers, is shown in Appendix 4. Rather than using lots of didactic teaching, tasks with sheets like these are designed to get the pupils to take more ownership of their learning. As described previously, the content can be cut and pasted from an A level specification into a Word document, then rearranged to produce the text for the speech bubbles. At this age, each group is usually self-chosen, with up to four members. All groups are asked to spend some time at the start to consider WAGOLL and success criteria and are then given up to three one-hour lessons and homework time to complete their tasks. Any early finishers can be assigned to help other groups (usually group 4, the experiment designers in this example).

Each group delivers their presentation, along with any handouts they have made, in 40 minutes (usually!), with the rest of the pupils making notes. The other 20 minutes of lesson time allows for discussion and debate, and for the teacher, when necessary, to intervene to correct errors and add other material. In this example, a further two lessons were given to allow group 4 to lead all the other pupils through the practical activities.

The total time needed from start to completion in the circulatory system example is around 10 to 12 hours, including practical work (not much different to the normal teaching time) but with far better retention of material for exams.

There are lots of opportunities for using your imagination to design similar choice sheets for Key Stage 3, 4 and all A level subjects.

Impressive projects – do a Berger!

Ron Berger, who we've met before, is now the chief academic officer for the non-profit school improvement network, Expeditionary Learning, which connects up project-based learning schools in the United States. Previously, he taught fifth or sixth grade in a small, rural US primary school. All the 'traditional' subjects were taught thematically through projects, some of which lasted for months at a time.

The hallmark of good projects, according to Berger, is the expectation that they will be done by the pupils with care, attention to detail and pride. In other words, with an ethic of excellence – hence the title of his excellent book (Berger, 2003).

Projects should be planned so that every child, of whatever ability, has a chance to succeed and produce work which is the best that they can do. This is achieved by:

- Devising some project components that all the pupils will do.

- Providing flexible optional components for faster workers.
- Producing checklists specifying completion dates for each aspect of a component, to be reviewed daily.
- Having clear success criteria for all components, often negotiated with the pupils.
- Building in literacy, numeracy and a cross-curricular approach.
- Teaching traditional skills-based and content-based lessons immediately prior to when they will be needed for each project.
- Providing professional-quality materials and teaching the pupils to respect them.
- Encouraging ownership by getting pupils to buy and use their own materials.
- Contacting experts for their help.
- Eventually sharing *all* projects with a wider audience – parents, the community, etc.

Berger describes some awesome and inspiring examples of science projects he has conducted, such as a radon study, for which his 10- to 12-year-old pupils investigated the levels of radon gas in their home town. In a project about water, they studied the purity of water in the local streams and lakes and then the well water used by houses in the town.

None of the material they needed was in school textbooks, so, 'We read published scientific papers, newspaper articles, government reports, informational pamphlets, and selections

from scientific books. We read professional scientific cata-
logues in order to order supplies and we read instructional
booklets explaining test kits' (Berger, 2003: 73). The pupils
measured parameters like pH, turbidity, nitrates and dis-
solved oxygen, using professional techniques and potentially
dangerous reagents to do so. Despite concerns, 'All the students, boys and girls alike, were meticulous in their respect
for and care of the testing equipment. In small, mixed-
gender, mixed-age teams, outfitted in goggles and gloves,
they worked with serious precision' (Berger, 2003: 111).

With Berger's help, the pupils wrote to, phoned and emailed
experts to ask them if they would visit the school to help
with and critique their work. They enlisted officers from the
water authorities, local councils, college students and enthusiastic professors, one of whom had a new machine (an
inductively coupled plasma mass spectrometer) which he put
at the disposal of the pupils to test water samples for metals.
When the experts visited the school, the pupils greeted them,
helped them to set up equipment, served them food and
drink and wrote to them afterwards, thanking them for their
help. The pupils also contacted homeowners explaining what
they wanted to do and why, and then carried out tests on
well water throughout the town.

Because the pupils knew that they were going to publish and
present the results at a public meeting, they knew they had
to work meticulously and professionally when collating the
results. They became experts in data analysis, graphing and
using spreadsheets. They took great care in presenting their

reports scientifically and in wording them carefully so that the public would understand their findings. Pupils prepared a report for the town council and local officials and each pupil wrote to a particular household detailing their findings and explaining how to address any concerns.[14]

A major stumbling block for most teachers, especially in primary schools, is that there isn't enough time to do this sort of project. They wonder how they will teach literacy, numeracy and the rest of the content of the national curriculum as well. If they reframe their thinking, these teachers might see that these can be taught *through* projects. In secondary schools, projects could be taught across and through maths and English lessons, as well as science – or, indeed, any other subject – given flexible thinking, a clear set of success criteria, a series of deadlines for tasks to be carried out in each lesson and so on. As Berger said to teachers worried about missing out content, 'Do I regret sacrificing the shallow coverage of countless facts in order for the students to craft something of excellence and importance? Not for a moment. Many of these students hope to become scientists. In fact, as Maria [a student] said to her fellow students, "We already are!"' (Berger, 2003: 116).

The new science national curriculum has an emphasis on 'working scientifically'; with some flexible thinking, much of it could be taught through extended projects. Well-planned projects can bring out all manner of hidden talents and

---

14 More details about Berger's project work can be found in White (2000). For an excellent introduction to project-based learning see: http://www.edutopia. org/project-based-learning.

abilities, provide opportunities to practise all of the learning habits and enrich the lives of pupils. Projects allow pupils to see that scientific knowledge is part of a larger picture. They also give a context and a purpose to the practical work the pupils do, and so help to maintain their interest and curiosity. The projects should be billed from the start as being something that will be presented to a wider audience, which will give the pupils an incentive to give their best effort, and assessment and imperative feedback (see below) can be built in.

Assessment as learning with feedback

Teachers *have* to assess progress, but the people who really *want* and *need* to assess progress are the pupils themselves.

A lot of teachers spend a lot of time thinking about how they can extract progress data either formatively or summatively from their pupils. So, they think up ways of questioning, testing, examining or otherwise assessing their pupils to get the data. So far, so good. But some teachers have a mindset which says assessment is something to be done *to* their pupils rather than done *with* them. They think of assessment as being mainly of benefit to the teacher, or the school or for reports to parents. Assessment does serve these uses, but it should not only be summative. Its primary purpose is to allow the pupils, working with their teachers, to improve their skills, knowledge and understanding.

Formative assessment should:

- Let pupils (and you) know what the pupils already know and understand (or not). ☑
- Demonstrate to them the goal they are aiming for (and WAGOLL). ☑
- Show them how to use success criteria to assess whether they have achieved the goal. ☑
- Give feedback to let them know if they have achieved the goal and/or what to do if they have not. ☑

It is easy to miss the fact that often, despite appearances, pupils really do *want* to know how well they are doing – how well they have understood a new concept, how well they are doing relative to their classmates. They have a *need* for this information so that they know where they stand in relation to their learning and their peers and so they know *what* they need to improve. They then need, with your help, further feedback to show them *how* to improve.

Too often, though, that last step gets missed or is done badly. So, for many pupils, assessment is not a shared learning experience. It is an exercise that gives them only a vague idea of how good or bad they are at something. They get taught stuff, they get tested, the teachers get their data and the class moves on to the next bit of stuff. Frequently, the pupils who need it may try asking for help but all too often too little or no help comes, because the class has to move on. This is the start of disillusionment for many pupils.

It doesn't have to be like this. With careful planning, assessment (followed, if possible, by immediate feedback) can maintain the interest and curiosity of pupils even through difficult work and promote trust and cooperation between them and their teachers.

Assessment can also give teachers great feedback about how their teaching is going.

Assessing understanding in lessons and acting on the feedback

You have a plan. It includes your lesson aims, objectives/targets, engaging tasks, proof activities and resources. There are links to literacy, numeracy, spiritual, moral, social and cultural development (SMSC)[15] and other subjects, as appropriate. You've got them hooked with a great short starter. You've put up the aims and explained what the lesson is about and where it sits in the learning journey. You've revealed the objectives and explained, demonstrated or co-designed the success criteria. Everyone knows what to do. The pupils are engaged, curious, eager and motivated to meet the learning challenges.

Or are they? Have you lost some of them already? Have you already baffled the class? If so, check back over the points covered under 'Be aware' (at the start of this chapter) for some possible reasons. This is highly relevant for both new

---

15 For more information about how Ofsted view SMSC see: http://www.schoolslinkingnetwork.org.uk/wp-content/uploads/2013/07/3-Spiritual-Moral-Social-and-Cultural-Definitions.pdf.

and experienced teachers. You may have developed habits over several years of teaching that you aren't aware of, so constant reflection on your impact is a lifelong professional requirement.

If pupils' answers, body language or behaviour indicate that they aren't following you, *act on the feedback!* Don't plough on regardless. Retrench and reframe your explanation. Praise those who understand, but also praise those who didn't understand and who let you know. Try to maintain a supportive environment.

Do some metacognition (page 117). Have you been properly checking their understanding since the beginning of the lesson? Or have you been asking, 'Do you understand?', or other vague questions, and blithely carrying on?

Seeing, hearing and circulating

Use your eyes and ears. This is the best and easiest way to get immediate feedback about pupils' engagement and understanding while you are starting, explaining or managing any class activity.

If you are speaking, they should be looking at you; so look for, and expect, eye contact.

- If they are tracking you with their eyes – they're interested.
- If they avoid your eyes when you're asking questions – they're not understanding.

- ▨ If they have eyes with a glazed look – they've gone to sleep!
- ▨ If they are looking into each other's eyes – their minds are elsewhere!

Check their body language. Are they slouching, fidgeting or otherwise going off task? If so, get them re-engaged as soon as possible. Remind them of your routines.

Own the room. Circulate widely and often to check their written work, give prompts, verbally reward or simply smile at them for good work. Listen to their conversations and discussions and check for understanding and use of key words. Never spend too long with one individual or group. Always use the eyes in the back of your head. This is especially true if they are doing practical work!

Good question!

How do *you* know that the pupils know and understand what they are doing and are making progress? Ask the pupils – endlessly! Make sure this becomes habitual. When questioning the pupils' understanding, make sure that:

- ▨ Your questions are clear, jargon-free, relevant and open. ☑
- ▨ You give less able pupils enough time to answer. ☑ (It's a fact that teachers give less able pupils less time than able pupils to respond before they jump in and give them the correct answer.)

- You question pupils of different abilities. ☑
- You never ask, 'Do you understand?' and just carry ☑
  on regardless.

If a pupil asks a question, thank them, repeat it, wait up to five seconds to let the question sink in – then ask other pupils to answer it.

Questioning strategies

No 'opt out'.[16] Use this always. If you ask a question, don't answer it yourself, thereby letting the pupil or the class opt out. If pupil X says, 'I don't know', do one of these four things:

1. Give pupil X a cue (e.g. a recently used phrase or symbol) or a clue (e.g. 'Remember when …').

2. Ask another pupil to do this.

3. Ask pupil Y for an answer, and go on asking others until you get a correct answer. Then get pupil X to repeat the correct answer in his or her own words. (If you find no one can answer, this is feedback to you showing you that need to rephrase either your question, original explanation or both.)

4. Give the answer and get pupil X to repeat it.

---

16 For more on this see Lemov (2009: 11).

Directly question individual pupils. Don't vaguely address questions to the whole class. And directly question pupils whether or not they have their hands up. Never allow shouting out of answers by anyone.

Have a 'no hands up' policy. There are lots of reasons for this: without one, quicker thinkers answer before slower ones have had a chance to think a question through; too many pupils hide behind others; pupils with their hands down might just be unsure but can't say so; and shy pupils are reluctant to volunteer to put their hands up. The 'no hands up' technique, used often, makes *all* the pupils pay attention. They will all have to mentally rehearse answers to all your questions in order not to be 'found out'. They can't let someone else do the work and stay in their comfort zones.

Think, pair, share. Ask a question, tell the pupils to pair up, think about the answer and discuss it together. You then ask pairs for their responses and ask other pairs to explain, justify or expand on the answers. This makes the learning safer as the discussion is just between the pair, not in front of everyone. Also, pairs come up with more ideas and it's easier for a pair to admit they don't know.

Yes/no questions. Bear in mind that they will be answered correctly 50% of the time by pupils who haven't got a clue!

Follow up pupils' answers (especially to yes/no questions) with supplementary 'Why?' or 'Can you explain how?' questions, which gauge not only knowledge but deeper understanding.

Randomise questioning. Use Lolly Lotto (names on lollipop sticks that you draw out) or have 'hot seats' with numbers under them, corresponding to a list of prepared questions or simply to the order in which you ask the children questions. Or fix numbered questions under their seats before pupils enter the room. Old hat, perhaps, but easy to do. (You could also give these out randomly as pupils enter the class.) There are also ICT tools for this.

Top tip

▨ Remember to treat pupils' answers as feedback ☑ on your teaching. Use this to alter your strategy or lesson plans going forward. Show that you are flexible and responsive to their needs.

Monitoring strategies or plenaries?

These are the same thing. A plenary is simply a strategy used at the end of a lesson to monitor progress (à la three-part lesson style). But don't wait until then to find out if the pupils have attained the lesson objectives or targets. Monitor progress as often as you can. You don't want to find out that no one understood the lesson until the pupils do a home-work or topic test or, even worse, when an observer tells you!

The strategies below can be used at any time in the lesson to monitor progress and gauge understanding:

▨ *Justify.* Frequently ask pupils who give correct answers to justify, expand on or explain their answer – that is, ask them to prove that they understand something. And ask those who admit that they don't understand why this is so. Use with the following strategies.

▨ *Thumbs up or thumbs down.* To indicate 'I understand' or 'I don't understand'. You can also have thumb level for 'not sure'.

▨ *Learning arrows.* Laminated arrow-shaped cards with a big paperclip slider on them which the pupils move to show their level of understanding.

▨ *Traffic lights.* The pupils have a red, amber and green card which they hold up or have on their desk, showing the colour that represents their level of understanding.

▨ *Learning continuums.* Where pupils physically place themselves along a wall between posters saying, for example, Agree/Disagree or Understand fully/Don't get it.

▨ *Human bar charts.* As for learning continuums, but with four or five levels of understanding. This can also be adapted to show responses to multiple choice questions in a fun way – and it gives you good feedback as to the pupils' understanding of the questions. Get the ones who get the right answer to pair up with and explain the answer to those that didn't.

▨ *Dry-wipe boards.* Use these to see the pupils' answers at a glance.

▓ *ICT.* There are various 'clicker' technologies to allow anonymous responses to your questions which let you see immediately how many pupils are on track.

▓ *Spoof assessments.* If you have been using critiques to determine success criteria, then give them a spoof assessment – a made-up or an anonymised piece of work done by a pupil in a previous year. Pupils mark this using the assessment criteria you have just determined to see if they understand them.

▓ *Differentiated proof activities.* These include answering prepared verbal or written questions, drawing an annotated diagram, producing a poster, setting up a circuit, giving a presentation and so on. Use them during the lesson and as homework to find out who has understood the individual objectives and the overall aim.

Strategies used at the end of a lesson could include:

▓ *Tapping the door frame.* Ask the pupils to tap high up, at waist height or low down as the they leave to show their level of understanding. A more useful version of this uses named sticky notes stuck to the frame.

▓ *Exit tickets.* Hand out 'tickets' to everyone towards the end of the lesson. Each ticket contains a few questions which test their understanding of the lesson objectives and the application of the knowledge to new contexts. Try to analyse them before the pupils leave by peer marking, if you have time, then collecting them in as the pupils leave. No ticket, no exit! Analyse them for common mistakes or misconceptions before the next lesson so you know what and how to prepare for it. Start the next lesson with the answers to the ticket or by taking some pupils aside. The tickets could also include a space for them to comment on the lesson and what they thought of your teaching, such as, 'What would you like me to keep, grow or change?'

If you can, at the end of the lesson make them wonder what is coming next. Give them tantalising glimpses of what is to come, pique their curiosity and interest. Get them hooked before they even start!

Know thy impact[17] (and let others see thy impact)

The assessment strategies described above will help you to know your impact, in terms of whether or not your pupils know, understand and can apply what you have taught them. But do all of them let others see your impact?

Ephemeral vs. tangible assessment evidence

When pupils answer questions orally or show you their traffic lights, you may see and hear that the pupils have made great progress in a lesson, but unless you videotape the lesson or an observer sees it, there is no hard evidence or proof. These are ephemeral assessments. They help pupils to progress but you can't use them to persuade others that you

---

17 These words were used by John Hattie to summarise the principles of his book, *Visible Learning for Teachers* (2012: 6).

have made an impact or, as Ofsted put it, show, 'pupils' academic achievement over time, taking account of both attainment and progress' (Ofsted, 2014a: 10).

You need tangible evidence which shows others (and the pupils themselves) the progress they have made as a result of your work with them. This is often very difficult, especially if you have only had a class for a short time. Tangible evidence might include:

- Summative assessment evidence: test and exam results, controlled practical assessment results, etc.
- Work in exercise books, on worksheets, etc.
- Posters, displays, models, etc. which the pupils have made.

These are tangible and can be shown to others, but do they, on their own, show progress over time? If not, maybe this evidence comes from the marking.

Pointless marking

Progress isn't evidenced or helped by mere 'flick and tick' marking, with occasional vapid comments like, 'Could do better', 'Poor effort', 'Good', 'Think!' or 'Use a pencil and a ruler'. As Ofsted observe:

> 'The most ineffective comments related to unfinished work; this was disappointingly common. Sometimes students do not complete a report, or record enough results to make any scientific conclusion valid, and there may well be a good reason why that is the case. But repeating the remark "Finish this off" suggests that neither the student nor the teacher was taking any notice of the marking.'
>
> Ofsted (2013: 32)

Low quality marking like this is a waste of time and any comments made are almost universally ignored.

Even long, well-written, potentially useful comments are ignored if they follow a grade – especially a poor one. It's really hard for pupils (or adults) to concentrate on good feedback if they are busy thinking that they are a failure.

Great marking with imperative feedback

> 'Consistently high quality marking and constructive feedback from teachers ensure that pupils make significant and sustained gains in their learning.'
>
> Ofsted (2014b: 61)

High quality marking:

- Is done against agreed success criteria, focusing on the learning objectives, skills and strategies used and habits for learning.

- Is appreciated and welcomed by the pupils (for more on developing a growth mindset see Chapter 4).

- Addresses literacy issues, not only the correct spelling of scientific terms.

- Comments on effort and progress over a number of attempts.

- Identifies good work.

- Identifies errors.

- Gives imperative feedback.

Imperative feedback doesn't just point out an error and simply say, 'This is wrong', or suggest, however helpfully, that the pupil might do something differently 'Next time ...'. Imperative feedback makes pupils focus again on the learning objectives and success criteria, on the effort they have made and the strategies they have used. Crucially, it then makes them *do something* to improve their work as a result of the feedback. It demands a response!

It takes time to mark well and give great feedback, so concentrate on a few pieces which will be marked in depth. But which pieces? Ofsted offer the following advice:

> 'The main difficulty is choosing what is worth marking diagnostically. Too often, students are set tasks or make notes that do not really allow them to reveal their understanding of a science concept or idea. Teachers should consider longer written activities, maybe taking several days, which allow students to research, think about and then apply their understanding of a science idea through a summary explanation.'
>
> Ofsted (2013: 32)

The choice sheets and projects discussed earlier in this chapter offer lots of scope. Look again at these and see how they could be used here.

When marking a piece of work, bear in mind the bullet points above and make your imperative feedback comments clear and specific. For example:

- Rewrite the last paragraph to include …
- Redraw and re-label the diagram using …
- Use all the key words in …
- Meet the success criteria for …
- To get to the next level you need to do …
- You missed … Include it here.

You can also use correction rubrics or symbols for common errors so that you don't end up writing more than the pupils did. For example:

- Underline misspellings in red with 'sp' in the margin (don't correct them – expect them to).
- A vertical line in the margin with an 'R' next to it means rewrite this section.
- An underlined sentence indicates a rewrite is necessary due to poor grammar.
- 'Kw' (with a tick sign) indicates the correct use of a key word (a cross means the opposite).
- Use ☺ for good work.

Speak to the English department or adapt the school marking policy to suit.

DIRT or 'critique' lessons

Dedicated improvement and reflection time (DIRT), a phrase first coined by Jackie Beere (2011: 29–30), is needed if pupils are to give your imperative feedback the attention it deserves. As the name implies, the pupils have to use your feedback or the success criteria (or both) to:

- Reflect on why their work did or didn't meet the success criteria.
- Reflect on the skills and strategies they used.
- Act on the imperative feedback.

Their reflections are best written down and should show that they have really thought about how they might improve against the success criteria. The pupils then act on your imperative feedback. This may involve them redrafting their work or parts of it.

Some DIRT lessons can be run with pupils peer assessing work. With good guidance about being kind, specific and helpful (see Berger et al., 2014: 171), pupils quickly learn to do this well, becoming expert at giving their peers imperative feedback against the success criteria and WAGOLL; feedback not only about the quality of presentation, but about the science. Deep learning!

Redrafting work – progress made plain

Consider how the pupils will redraft their work when planning how they will write it up. Doing this sort of work in exercise books may not be a good idea, so create specific DIRT folders instead.

Get the pupils to begin by writing their piece of work on alternate lines on one side of a sheet of paper. This leaves space for them to write in their corrections and improvements. Get them into the mindset that this is a work in progress – that the first draft will not be the finished piece, that the second draft may also require some improvement and that it may be only the third draft which is the finished piece.

Pin the drafts and completed work side by side on your wall. Keep them in plain view of any visitor. The evidence that you help your pupils to make progress and take pride in what they do will be plain to see.

The video of Austin's butterfly is a classic example of redrafting in action, in which Ron Berger explains to primary school pupils of two different ages how to critique their work.[18] He uses the example of a first grade (6-year-old) boy called Austin who has to produce an accurate, scientific drawing of a butterfly. Listen out for the habits of outstanding learners and Berger's use of the word 'yet'. Think about how this sort of redrafting could be used in your science lessons.

Planning lessons and schemes of work

When we are planning the learning journey, we shouldn't only be concerned with teaching the content of science. We should also be planning to develop in our pupils the skills, attributes and habits to enable them to become outstanding lifelong learners.

The figure below shows how each part of the learning journey described so far in Chapter 2 fits with the others. It also shows how the parts of a lesson should relate to and develop the dispositions for outstanding learning found in the bottom

---

18 See: http://elschools.org/student-work/austins-butterfly-drafts. Scroll to the bottom of the page to find the video, then explore the Expeditionary Learning website for more good ideas and materials.

box. (Chapter 4 deals with these dispositions and how they might be taught.)

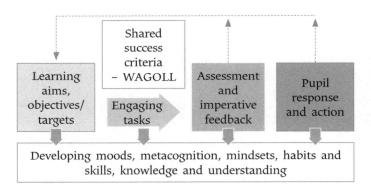

Source: © Jackie Beere Associates.

You know your curriculum time and what content you have to teach. Don't forget to include these dispositions in your planning if you want your pupils to learn how to learn and, as a result, increase their motivation to become better scientists.

An A4 version of the following diagram could be used to quickly summarise a lesson plan for yourself or for a visitor. The more experienced a teacher you are, the less you will have to write.

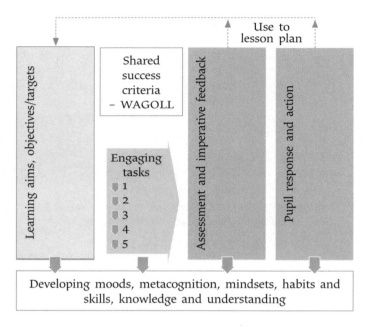

Source: © Jackie Beere Associates.

Planning using sheets like this means that whole schemes can be summarised quickly. You can also keep in clear sight the important aspects of what you are trying to teach and won't get bogged down in or lose the plot among the details of a lesson plan. (Detailed lists of apparatus would be kept separate from these planning sheets.)

This outline plan works in the following way:

- *The arrows* at the top of the diagram serve as a reminder to link the learning to the previous lesson and to prior learning.

- *The success criteria* are shown at the top of the diagram so that you concentrate on getting the pupils to meet these.

- *The tasks* within the lesson may be central to the lesson (and the sheet), but please remember that they are merely the vehicle which enables the pupils to demonstrate progress.

- *The assessment box* is to encourage you to think about particular questions you might ask and to consider what other strategies, such as homework, you might use to evidence progress. After the lesson, you could also record here any feedback you had to give which was common to a lot of the pupils (and to whom).

- *The pupil response and action* box could be filled in after the lesson or after marking work from the lesson. In it you can summarise the feedback and begin to plan the next lesson based on this (e.g. Which aspects of the lesson might you have to repeat (and why)? With whom? How you plan to do this – whole class or working with a group?).

- *The dispositions box* is for you to list the skills and other attributes you might expect the pupils to develop in the lesson (and how).

Please feel free to adapt this plan as you wish. You can also find a different method of lesson planning designed by Ross McGill, called the 5 Minute Lesson Plan, at the very popular @TeacherToolkit website.[19] For other thoughts on planning science lessons, and topics covered here and elsewhere, see Tom Sherrington's very useful book, *Teach Now! Science* (2014).

---

19   See: http://teachertoolkit.me/the-5-minute-lesson-plan/.

Chapter 3
Moving Towards Outstanding Teaching

Try to answer this question truthfully:

Do your pupils feel that your lab or classroom is a positive, exciting learning environment?

The answer to this apparently simple question actually has many components; so many, in fact, that the full answer takes up the rest of this book! I will try to deal with each component in turn, some of which are obvious, some are not. Some will take a paragraph or two to explain, some may take a whole chapter, some have had whole books written about them.

The purpose of this book is to ensure that the answer to the question is a resounding 'yes!' and to suggest some strategies that will help your pupils (and you) to make expected or better progress. And if your pupils are doing that, then you don't need to worry about being observed or inspected.

The learning environment

Any classroom or lab environment is primarily made up of the interaction of teacher (and her planning), the pupils in the class and the physical environment. Less immediate are interactions with other factors, such as the school ethos, attainment and the socio-economic context of the school.

The most important interaction is, of course, the pupil–teacher relationship. You are there to direct and lead the learning and set the tone in your classroom or lab. You will use your subject knowledge and lesson planning skills to teach the subject content.

For most pupils, however, your subject knowledge is of minor concern, at least at first. Their prime concern is about what you are like – how you set up and maintain pupil–teacher relations. They are exquisitely sensitive to how you interact with them and are very quick to form lasting opinions about you that can be hard to change, so we will deal with this first.

What pupils look for in outstanding pupil–teacher relationships

What pupils think about science

Whenever we talk to children about what makes their science (or any other) lessons great, the first replies they give are always linked to the attributes (and foibles) of their teachers.

Here are some examples of comments that pupils have made when asked about their science teachers:

- We've got Miss X – she always makes her lessons fun.
- He's kind of strict, but good.
- Miss is just brilliant. I just *so* get her lessons.
- He really listens to us and helps us lots if we're stuck.
- She cares about us and about our learning.
- He knows his stuff and explains it well.
- We know he wants us all to do well and he shows us how to do it.
- She always makes my brain hurt – in a good way.

Comments about the science they are taught almost always come second – if they get a mention at all! Sometimes, with some prompting about what they actually do in science lessons, pupils say how science is so inspiring and so interesting. They say how the 'stuff' (facts, terminology, concepts) they have learned explain so much about what they see and do, and how their bodies work and how to look after them. Older pupils sometimes talk about how science fits with other subjects, how it encourages new ways of thinking, enriches their lives and opens up excellent career paths.

But not all pupils agree. For far too many pupils, science is seen as boring – as just a lot of stuff to learn. Many children (particularly in secondary schools) have become disengaged and think negatively about science and science teaching. For them the 'fun' has gone out of it. The people who make science live or die for pupils are their teachers.

Listen to pupils discussing new timetables. The first question they ask each other about any subject is, 'Who have you got next year?' (Wouldn't it be great if you overheard that they were really glad to have you!) But what do pupils base judgements like this on? What criteria do they use to decide whether or not they like a particular teacher?

Whether we like it or not, our pupils are extremely sensitive to what they see their teachers do, what they hear their teachers say and how their teachers make them feel. Within a couple of lessons, pupils will have rated their teachers based on these observations. So, what is it that they are looking and listening for?

What pupils see: non-verbal behaviours

Pupils look for:

- How often the teacher smiles.
- Whether they have open body language and open gestures.
- How often the teacher makes eye contact.
- If the teacher moves around the room.
- If the teacher has a relaxed body posture.
- How assertive the teacher appears.

■ The teacher's appearance, including how they are dressed.

Within as short a time as two seconds, pupils will begin to use these cues to rate how confident the teacher seems and will have started to decide whether or not they like what they see. As Malcolm Gladwell found, 'A person watching a silent two-second video clip of a teacher he or she has never met will reach conclusions about how good that teacher is that are very similar to those of a student who has sat in the teacher's class for an entire semester' (Gladwell, 2005: 13).

What pupils hear: methods of communication

Pupils listen for the teacher's accent, dialect, tone, pitch and volume of voice. If none of these prove too distracting, they will go on to listen to the vocabulary being used, as well as:

■ How intelligible that vocabulary is.

■ How the teacher uses (or overuses) praise and what they are praising pupils for (see Chapter 4 for more on praise).

■ How assertive the teacher sounds.

■ If what is being said gives any clue about how 'friendly' (or, as we might say, how empathetic) the teacher is.

At first, pupils don't listen so much to *what* you are saying, as to *how* you are saying it. Later, they will put this together with what they see to come to judgements about how the teacher makes them feel.

What pupils feel: emotional responses

Using these visual and auditory cues, pupils will very quickly assess how much empathy and rapport the teacher seems to have with them and their classmates. In other words, pupils will ask:

- Can this teacher see the lesson from my point of view?
- Does she see the difficulties I and others may have?
- How does he deal with pupils who misunderstand? Does he deal with them kindly and sympathetically?
- Does she seem 'nice'?

In other words:

- Is this a safe place to learn?
- Can I take the risk of getting it wrong in this class?

This sets up a picture in the pupils' minds about how well, or not, they might get on with the teacher. We use the same cues to judge other people – and also come to conclusions about them in minutes. Pupils have hours and hours to draw conclusions about their teachers. We make them sit there and do so!

After a couple of lessons, pupils will also have judged whether or not the teacher:

- Seems fair and understanding.
- Has favourites.
- Sets clear routines.

▓ Sees and disciplines consistently those who don't cooperate.

▓ Deals well with classroom routines (particularly how they organise and supervise practical work).

▓ Has a passion for their subject.

Above all, the pupils will judge how well the teacher and the lessons they plan engage them. (There is much more about getting great engagement in your lessons later in this chapter.)

All pupils judge and rate teachers. But if you ask them *how* they do it, many struggle because they do so unconsciously based on visual and aural clues. Pupils also rate their lessons ('That was rubbish/great'). Again, if asked, many would struggle to find the words to describe why they came to the judgement they did. This is because they haven't been taught a language for learning with which to express themselves (see Chapter 4 for more on this).

Do you know what your pupils think about you (and science)?

Do you know, or *think* you know, the answers to these questions? Have you invited evaluation from your pupils and colleagues? Do you know your pupils' perceptions about science? If not, why not? Do you think there is too little time to find out, or is there some other reason? Surely, the last thing you want is to find out the answers to these questions from your line manager or an Ofsted inspector!

Knowing what others think is crucial to effective self-evaluation and, therefore, to progressing your teaching. You may have theories about what others think of you, but, as we say in science, you can't make valid conclusions without the evidence. An example questionnaire that you could use to find out your students' views about your teaching appears in Appendix 1. Let your pupils know that you are using the results of the questionnaire to set targets for your teaching. If your coaching session has led to decisions which involve trying a new strategy in class, let the pupils in on it and ask them to help you gauge its success. Practice what you preach!

We give lots of feedback to our pupils and expect them to act on it. So, no matter what career stage we are at, we should model that we seek feedback; that we don't melt down if it's bad; that we are responsive to it and see it as a challenge to improve.

If the answers to the questionnaire are all positive – great! Let everyone know and include it in a portfolio of evidence of good practice. If not, don't sit alone and dwell on the bad feedback. It's too easy to beat yourself up, despair and then, after the initial self-flagellation, start attributing blame elsewhere or thinking of excuses. If you don't want to be unpleasantly surprised by feedback, then use a range of methods to regularly ask your pupils whether they enjoyed your lessons. Try focus groups, suggestion boxes, class blogs and exit tickets (see page 82) to monitor attitudes alongside outcomes.

When you get some negative feedback, which we all will from time to time, be determined to think of it as an opportunity to improve – have a growth mindset about it (see pages 128–131). Ask yourself immediately where you can get help. When you do get help, focus on one issue at a time and focus on how you will move forward. To get the most benefit, use a peer coaching model such as the iSTRIDE model (described in Beere and Broughton (2013: 113) and outlined in Appendix 2). When, as a result of the process, your teaching improves, include this in your portfolio as evidence of self-reflection and progress. After all, the teacher should be the best learner in the class.

What makes an outstanding science teacher?

What follows is not an exhaustive list of the attributes of outstanding teachers – you could almost certainly add more – but it does summarise many of the qualities identified by John Hattie in his must-read book, *Visible Learning for Teachers* (2012: 25–32).

Outstanding teachers foster excellent pupil–teacher relationships. These contribute to a positive learning environment because:

- Outstanding teachers have an unswerving belief that they can make a difference for every one of their pupils.
- They are relentlessly curious learners (like you – you're reading this book!).

- They are curious about the process of learning and how to improve the learning experiences of their pupils.

- They are persistent, resilient and don't give up.

- They are great communicators – they are able, through explanation and demonstration, to make abstract concepts concrete.

- They are innovative and willing to take risks, trying new strategies and materials.

- They respond to feedback about what is happening in their classrooms and welcome feedback about their teaching.

- They actively teach their pupils metacognitive strategies and about the moods, mindsets and habits of great learners, encouraging them to learn how to learn.

- They have a store of strategies and expert subject knowledge which they can adapt to meet the needs of their pupils.

- They can anticipate and empathise with the difficulties their pupils may have.

- They are great questioners – they are able to use questions to assess and enhance progress and dispel misconceptions.

- They are great listeners.

- They are keen observers of learning in the classroom, spotting misconceptions and intervening with pupils who need help.

▨ They don't dominate the learning process but involve the pupils in it.

▨ They praise effort much more than outcomes.

▨ They foster a safe, trusting, considerate learning environment in which there is unconditional support for all and in which it is alright to take a risk and fail.

▨ They have routines (see page 33).

▨ They are consistent in the application of sanctions and rewards.

▨ They have high expectations and encourage high aspirations among their pupils.

▨ They are passionate, knowledgeable and enthusiastic about their subject.

▨ They plan great lessons.

▨ They ensure that lesson objectives and/or learning intentions are met.

▨ They are role models for their pupils.

▨ They know their impact.

▨ They work with teaching assistants, other adults and their colleagues to share good practice and to help nurture all the above attributes in them.

▨ They probably also walk on water.

If these attributes are not innate (yet), don't worry. You'll be pleased to know that you can learn to develop them all (except, perhaps, the last one!). As you will discover in the section on mindsets for learning in Chapter 4, if you cultivate what Carol Dweck (2006: 16) describes as a growth mindset, you really can change. Indeed, she believes it is only people with a growth mindset who can learn to truly change.

In the spirit of self-reflection, which of the above attributes are strengths for you? Which could do with some work, and how might you go about it?

Lesson planning to engage

If you have the attributes outlined above, then you are a long way down the road towards creating a positive learning environment. In turn, these characteristics will influence and be reflected in how you plan and deliver lessons.

Engaging lessons, and the tasks within them, are absorbing because they engage the emotional brain. They will incorporate many of these elements:

- Novelty or surprise
- Humour
- Music
- Rhythm/rhyme
- Love
- Mystery
- Stories
- Passion

For a really good book full of engaging strategies, try the aptly named *Outstanding Teaching: Engaging Learners* (Griffith and Burns, 2012).

To engage their pupils, outstanding teachers:

- Plan lessons and sequences of lessons with challenging goals accompanied by clear success criteria and dedicated time for feedback.
- Link the lesson content with other subject knowledge and aid the pupils' spiritual, moral, and cultural development.
- Secure immediate engagement and sustain it throughout the lesson and sequences of lessons by using a wide range of absorbing, relevant, practical and other activities.
- Explicitly teach their pupils to understand metacognition and the moods, mindsets and habits of effective learners, and plan opportunities for doing this into their lessons.
- Create opportunities for dialogue, discussion and plenaries to gauge the learning progress.
- Carefully plan feedback (which should always be imperative – see page 85) into lessons or sequences of lessons, making the pupils respond in some way.
- Check that their pupils act on feedback to ensure that they are making progress and are gaining lasting, deep knowledge.
- Plan homework, if any, to enhance, reinforce or test understanding. It is never an add-on.

- Do not plan lessons, or teach, to a set format – they do what works to help their pupils to progress.
- Do not write out massive and exhaustive plans which take hours to do (and which no one reads properly).

The last two points are important. As Her Majesty's Chief Inspector, Michael Wilshaw (2014) said, 'This is clear and unequivocal. We are putting power firmly in the hands of the classroom teacher to determine how they should teach. We do not – let me repeat, not – have any preferred teaching style.' This is also made clear in the Inspection Handbook, which states:

> 'Inspectors must not advocate a particular method of teaching or show preference towards a specific lesson structure. As such, inspectors will not look for a preferred methodology but must record aspects of teaching that are effective and identify ways in which teaching and learning can be improved. ... inspectors must not advocate a particular approach to teaching or planning lessons. It is for the school to determine how best to teach and engage pupils to secure their good learning.'
>
> Ofsted (2014b: 10–11)

And as for lesson plans:

'Inspectors will not expect teachers to prepare lesson plans for the inspection.'

Ofsted (2014b: 16)

Which is not to say that they don't expect you to have a plan for the lesson! It means that they don't want (or need) voluminous, step-by-step plans. (An outline such as the one on page 92 would be sufficient.)

If your teaching and planning is close to that described in the previous two lists of bullet points, you will have covered the grade descriptors for what Ofsted judge to be outstanding teaching (see Ofsted, 2014b: 61). You will also have covered what Ofsted have to say about the role of teaching:

'The most important role of teaching is to promote learning and the acquisition of knowledge by pupils and to raise achievement. It is also important in promoting the pupils' spiritual, moral, social and cultural development. Teaching includes:

■ planning for lessons and learning activities at other times in the school day

- how teachers impart knowledge to pupils, instruct them and engage them in other activities which also increase their knowledge and understanding
- the setting of appropriate, regular homework across subjects
- marking, assessment and feedback.

It encompasses activities within and outside the classroom, such as additional support and intervention. The quality of teaching received by pupils who attend off-site alternative provision should also be considered and evaluated.'

Ofsted (2014b: 57)

Additionally, if you and your colleagues develop these attributes and learn to plan and teach consistently in this way, you will begin to transform the attitudes and behaviours of your pupils.

Pupils' responses to outstanding teaching and planning

Pupils will respond (eventually!) to teachers who teach and plan as described above. They will respect you for being caring, engaging, knowledgeable and for being someone who helps them to learn how to learn. Your pupils will also see you as someone who helps them to understand that their lessons assist them in:

- Developing a thirst for knowledge and a love of learning.
- Taking pride in their work.
- Having respect for themselves and for others as learners.
- Developing the moods, mindset and habits which will serve them long into the future.
- And, yes, helping them to pass exams.

You will also have cultivated what Ofsted describe in their grade descriptors as outstanding behaviour and safety of pupils at the school (see Ofsted (2014b: 44)).

The physical environment

A positive learning environment is crucial to great progress, and a major component of this is the physical environment of the classroom.

Take another look at the lab or classroom you teach in. Check its physical condition, the displays, how the room is set out and used and look out keenly for any health and safety issues. Better still, get someone else with a fresh pair of eyes to do it for you. Invite them to answer as many of these questions as they can and ask you the rest:

The room and facilities

- Does it look welcoming and conducive to learning?
- Is it tidy or are there piles of books and equipment lying around?
- Is all the apparatus stored neatly?
- Does it work?
- Do you know where everything is?
- Can others find things easily?
- Are cupboards labelled?
- Are their contents used, or are they storing rubbish?
- Are the gas taps and electric sockets working?
- Are the sinks clean, with working taps and clean traps?
- Are the windows clean, inside and out?
- What is the paintwork like?
- Do the lights work?
- What is the ventilation like?
- Is it warm in winter and cool in summer (even with practical work going on)?
- Is there a large enough area to do demonstration work with the pupils close enough to see?
- Do any pupils have to do written or practical work facing away from you?
- Are there any potential hazards?
- Is there enough seating?

▨ Does the arrangement of the furniture allow for individual and group work? ☑

▨ Can you and the pupils move easily around the room? ☑

Your contributions

▨ Do you have posters, models, mobiles, etc. on display? ☑

▨ Are they relevant to what you are teaching now, or are they ageing relics? ☑

▨ Are there displays of exemplar work? ☑

▨ Are they recent? ☑

▨ Do they show feedback, pupil responses to it and progress? ☑

▨ Are key words on display? If so, are they used (and spelled correctly!)? ☑

▨ Are your (or the school's) aims on display? ☑

▨ Are there any motivational posters? ☑

▨ Do you make full use of your interactive whiteboard, if supplied? ☑

▨ Can everyone see it properly? ☑

▨ Do you have a large whiteboard area for you and your pupils to work on? ☑

▨ Do you have supplies of stationery, writing and drawing equipment? ☑

▨ Is there any IT present or available, such as   ☑
  dataloggers? If so, is it used?

Do you make good use of your lab assistants? They are in and around your lab and can give you feedback about how your room or lab might be improved and how your lessons work. They can give advice on maintenance, set-up and clearing of equipment during lessons and often have a wealth of interesting ideas about resources for supporting learning. Show them you value them by involving them in lessons. They have lots of skills and expertise to offer.

Finally, have you asked for any feedback about the learning environment from your pupils, and have you asked them to help you improve it? Challenge *them* to improve the environment. Get them to bring in plants or even animals (which they agree to be responsible for). Get them to regularly photograph experiments, apparatus, activities and so on, and display their efforts along with a report on what they were doing.

Beware! Don't get too carried away improving the physical environment and spend too much time on it at the expense of creating great lessons for the pupils!

Chapter 4
Moving Towards Outstanding Learning

When people think of what goes on in school they might say:

Teachers teach and pupils learn.

But this is only partly true. To be more accurate about what happens in the best of today's classrooms and labs we should say:

Teachers teach and learn and pupils learn and teach.

In fact, the teacher should be the best learner in the classroom and model this at all times. Outstanding teachers do this, and they also teach and model the moods, habits and mindsets which will promote outstanding lifelong learning in their pupils.

Moods, metacognition, habits and risk

The mood for learning

Ask your pupils this question at the start of a lesson:

What sort of mood are you in right now? Scale it from 1 (despair) to 10 (ecstatic). What number are you on?

Then say:

You've now got 30 seconds to turn to your neighbour and put him or her in a better mood. Go![1]

Within seconds the classroom comes alive with animated conversation and laughter. There are smiles on everyone's faces, the energy in the room spirals up and it can be difficult to make yourself heard. After the hubbub has quietened, ask what mood number your pupils are on now. Invariably it's higher. When asked how they now feel, pupils say they feel more positive, energetic, enthused, motivated and optimistic. Just the thought of putting someone else in a good mood has changed the atmosphere and, in addition, made the pupils realise the power they have to influence each other's moods.

They have a buzz and so are in a better mood for learning![2] Do this occasionally and link it to the rest of this chapter.

---

1   Adapted from Beere (2007: 39).
2   This finding was confirmed by Nadler et al. (2010) who saw a marked increase in cognitive flexibility – defined as the ability to seek out and apply alternate strategies to problems and to find unusual relationships between items – when subjects were in a positive mood.

Chapter 4

Metacognition

The following exercise can be used to introduce pupils to metacognition – often described as 'cognition about cognition' or 'knowing about knowing'. Jackie Beere (2014: 5) calls it 'thinking on purpose'.

It is very unusual for pupils to be asked to take a step back from themselves and think about things such as why they are in the mood they are in, how they might improve it and how mood impacts on their relationships and on their learning. If they understand mood – how it is, in fact, under their control and its importance in these contexts – you can go on and encourage them to:

- Self-judge themselves as learners by thinking metacognitively about why they are 'stuck' in lessons.
- Think about how they know whether they have met success criteria and what to do if they haven't.
- Think about resources and strategies they can use to overcome learning barriers.[3]
- Think about how to apply these resources and strategies and consider how effective they are.
- Deal with and learn from mistakes.
- Respond positively to feedback.
- Reduce distractions.

---

3 A range of these strategies need to be taught – and learned and practised. Pupils often start with a limited range of learning strategies which may not be effective.

▓ Raise their aspirations.

▓ Value effort over outcomes.

▓ Know that practice makes perfect.

▓ Recognise how and when to work with others.

▓ Develop a language with which they can describe their own learning.

In other words, you can begin to teach them about learning to learn. John Hattie (2012: 121–124, 269) describes how metacognition, or what he calls self-regulation strategies, is a vital component in learning and has one of the largest effects on outcomes. This finding is also supported by the Sutton Trust and the Education Endowment Foundation.[4]

Communication

If pupils use metacognition to stand back from their learning and learn from it, they also need a vocabulary to describe what, how and why they have studied.

The terminology for the 'what' will often come from the learning aims or objectives, the success criteria or even a list of key words. To describe the 'how' pupils need to be able to list the strategies and skills they have used. They should then be able to describe which ones worked well, or less well, why this was so and what they will try next time. The answer to the 'why' comes from the lesson aims and possibly from

---

4   See: http://educationendowmentfoundation.org.uk/toolkit/
    meta-cognitive-and-self-regulation-strategies/ for a summary of the cost and
    effectiveness of self-regulation (and lots of other) strategies.

overarching long-term aims, such as being able to link up different areas of their learning.

The pupils need this language so that they can self-assess or peer assess accurately and have better learning conversations with you. It also helps when you have an inquisitive visitor. Imagine having a visitor who asks a GCSE pupil about what she has been learning in the lesson. Wouldn't it be great if she replied with something like:

The overall aim is to understand recycling of materials in nature but today we've been looking at how carbon is recycled. Our group is putting together a detailed step-by-step flow chart. Eventually it will show how a carbon atom in CO_2 can pass through a plant leaf, get fixed in glucose in photosynthesis and eventually be respired and returned to the atmosphere by someone like me. I'm just doing the plant leaf bit – CO_2 in the air, through a stoma into an air space, into the moist surface of a palisade cell and so on … My friends are doing other parts of the process, then we'll check each other's work and put it together before presenting it to the class next lesson. Today we've pulled together processes like combustion, respiration, photosynthesis, digestion and decomposition and seen how they're all linked. We can see now how chemical reactions we learned about earlier underpin all these processes. This has really shown me that photosynthesis and respiration are like opposite chemical reactions.

It's a far cry from, and far more impressive than, 'I dunno'. The more that pupils give mini-presentations, debate, self-assess against criteria and are asked to explain their answers more fully, the more fluent their learning language becomes.

The habits of outstanding learners

Take a moment to think about the perfect pupil; not necessarily the most gifted, but the pupil you know will give of his or her best. What habits and attributes do these pupils have? When teachers and pupils are asked this question they come up with words like:

Alert	Motivated	Reliable
Being clever	Neat workers	Resilient
Communicative	Observant	Responsive to feedback
Critical	Optimistic	
Curious	Outgoing	Risk-taking
Enthusiastic	Perceptive	Sits still
Fast to finish	Personable	Sociable
Flexible	Positive	Stable
Honest	Questioning	Thorough
Listens well	Quiet	Well-behaved

Ask yourself, your colleagues and your pupils, which five habits do you think are the most important? Which five do you think are most often said by pupils?[5]

Now think about what percentage of your pupils show these five important habits. Do you think the percentage increases or decreases with age?

Now think about what percentage of your staff show the habits! Do *you* do so?

Are the great learning habits innate or are they learned behaviours? Most people would argue that they are a mixture of both. Young children are innately resilient – watch toddlers learning to walk; they will try, try and try again. The same resilience is revealed when their innate curiosity drives them to explore the world through their senses, or when they learn language – they use it to endlessly question others to satisfy their curiosity. But all of these abilities need encouragement and positive reinforcement to continue to develop.

Do the learning habits die?

Think about the average 3-year-old and the average 13-year-old. Which one is the most curious, most resilient, most open to advice, most willing to take a chance in class, most likely to be more communicative and ask more questions? The

---

5   Based on informal feedback to the author and editor at teacher conferences and in schools, the five most important habits overall were: curious, resilient, responsive to feedback, risk-taking and communicative. The habits most often selected by pupils were: being clever, fast to finish, listens well, sits still and neat workers.

answer is clearly the 3-year-old. The notable exceptions among the 13-year-olds will be the 'perfect' pupils who have somehow retained these habits.

It's remarkable, and disappointing, to see the decline in learning habits as pupils get older. As a result of losing the five most important habits, as well as other good learning habits, there is a perception that the older the pupils get, the more dependent they become on their teachers. Just ask any primary school teacher to describe the difference between Year 2 and Year 6 pupils or secondary teachers to do the same for Year 7 and Year 11 pupils. By Year 11, large numbers of children have become so disengaged, disorganised, disinterested and discouraged that they have to be pushed and pulled through their exams.

Ron Berger says the same of US schools:

'An enthusiastic attitude toward learning, made explicit through participating in class discussions and activities and showing excitement for ideas, seems universal in all the Kindergartens I visit across America, whether in poor or wealthy districts. It is *normal* to say you like school and learning. By secondary school, things are very different in many of the schools I visit. ... Many students related that you would be out of your mind to show interest in school or raise your hand in class. If you want to fit in you are crazy to let on that you care about your work.'

Berger (2003: 36)

If most teachers agree that the great learning habits are fundamental for great learning, then what is school doing to pupils? What happens to cause this loss of learning habits, and how can we avoid it?

Negative peer pressure and supportive environments

As they get older, pupils become much more aware of peer-to-peer interactions. If the dominant pupils in the class convey to others that 'it's not cool to learn', use words like 'boff', 'nerd' and 'geek', laugh at pupils who try or, worse, laugh at those who try and get it wrong, then you must confront this.

Be aware that pupils who do this usually do so because they are insecure about their ability to learn or have fixed mindsets about their ability (see below). However, some do it just to be mean. If you see this, intervene. Be absolutely clear about having zero tolerance of any negative peer pressure.

Try to find out about the root causes of these pupils' behaviours, and whether they are due to low self-esteem or something else. Determine whether these pupils need lessons on empathy or basic subject skills and knowledge, the value of education, the importance of the habits or a combination of all these.

But don't try to fix the whole school's problems all on your own. Let others know what you are doing, with whom, and enlist their help. And always tell others about anything you find out which has any relevance to safeguarding. Don't keep secrets!

Try asking your pupils, 'What do you have to do to fit in here?' Listen very carefully to their answers. Many will reveal what the learning atmosphere is like in the school for pupils. Again, don't try to fix the whole school's problems on your own. Discuss what you find out with others.

You need to make your classroom or lab into an environment where there is unconditional support for each other; where you expect excellence in effort from everyone, no matter what their ability. Be clear that if any pupil is failing to succeed, or shows a lack of pride in what they do, it is a concern for *everyone* in the room.

Try to use peer pressure positively. Get pupils into the habit of giving positive feedback to your difficult pupils, praising their good work and applauding their effort.

Discouragement and teaching learning habits

The environment beyond the classroom often has an even greater influence on whether good learning habits develop or are lost. If it is supportive, encouraging, stimulating and loving, the valuable habits and attributes will develop and continue to flourish. If it isn't, they often wither and wane. The withering of learning habits in disaffected children is often due to a lack of stimulus and encouragement, and is sometimes due to active discouragement. Some parents, and even some tired teachers, are guilty of this ('Stop asking those stupid questions!').

Loss of learning habits leads to a lack of understanding in lessons and, in turn, leads pupils to think negatively: 'I can't do this' or 'I'm no good at this'. This sets off a vicious cycle, ultimately leading to disengagement from learning. Somehow the 'perfect' pupils, often against the odds, manage to resist this. Perhaps, over the years, they have learned and re-learned resilience, massive self-belief, determination and optimism. Unfortunately, they are rarer than we would like – but we can change this. If habits can be learned, they can also be taught.

Teachers of science are uniquely positioned to be able to help teach about the importance of good learning habits, as this involves basic knowledge about how the brain works, cognitive psychology, neuroscience, developmental biology – all subjects that with the right approach are interesting and accessible to all.

Schools have pupils for about 1,000 hours per year – roughly 20% of their waking lives. Teaching learning habits in some of this time can markedly affect the other 80%.

If science teaching takes up 20% of curriculum time we have around 200 hours a year to help model, teach and grow the habits.

Teachers need to recognise the importance of teaching these habits. Who wouldn't want a classroom full of 'perfect' pupils (and better outcomes)? The habits can be planned into lessons and taught across the curriculum, but for this to be successful they must be modelled.

The importance of role models

Children need role models. If they don't find them at home, you may be their only chance. Outstanding teachers model excellent learning habits and attributes in their classroom and actively teach their pupils about fostering them – look again at the attributes of outstanding teachers in Chapter 3.

There are role models for the habits of great learners amongst famous scientists too. For example, Einstein, who developed the theory of relativity working as a patent clerk, the Curies, Stephen Hawking and the thousands of scientists and engineers at CERN who collaborated to find the Higgs boson.[6]

Learning is risky – staying in the comfort zone

As the cognitive scientist Daniel Willingham (2009: 4) said, 'The mind is not designed for thinking.' By 'thinking' he meant, 'solving problems, reasoning, reading something complex, or doing any mental work that requires some effort'. He also argues that people don't really want to think – it's hard work, takes energy and has uncertain outcomes. We could get it wrong and be punished in some way, be made fun of or lose self-esteem. So, learning is risky.

For most people, avoiding failure is more motivational than being successful. This is why most pupils, most of the time, are passive in lessons. They don't want to get engaged in the learning as thinking is hard *and* it's risky. They want to stay in their comfort zone. Our job is to get pupils out of their comfort zone and into the challenge zone. We have to get them to think.

A supportive learning environment removes the risk. But this alone won't get the pupils to invest the energy needed to really think about the lesson content, practise the learning habits and use metacognitive strategies to become outstanding learners. That is what outstanding lessons can do – providing also that the pupils have the right mindset for learning.

---

6 See: http://www.usasciencefestival.org/schoolprograms/2014-role-models-in-science-engineering/367-all-role-models.html for a searchable list of role models.

Mindsets for learning

This section is based on the work of Carol Dweck and her classic book, *Mindset: The New Psychology of Success* (2006). It is important because it shows that intelligence is not fixed, that how we praise pupils is crucial to their future success and that effort brings rewards.

The fixed mindset

Ask your pupils and, perhaps, some of your colleagues the following questions:

- Do you think that your ability is fixed at birth?
- Do you think that you have to constantly prove your ability to others and yourself?
- Do you think that failure is a setback?
- Do you think that success is about proving you are smart?
- Do you think that having to work hard at something shows you aren't clever?

If the answer to these questions is 'yes', then they probably have what Dweck calls a fixed mindset.

Mindsets develop when children begin to evaluate themselves, even as early as 4 years old (Dweck, 2006: 16). Some bright children compare themselves to others and realise that, without much effort, they are smart or talented at something. This is good, but what they then do is put themselves on a pedestal. They think and say things like, 'Smart people shouldn't have to work hard to succeed' or 'Smart people don't fail.' And, crucially, when in school, they may feel, 'People are watching me or looking at or measuring what I do. I cannot fail as they might think I'm stupid.' As a result, when faced with the choice of easier or more difficult problems to solve, they tend to choose the easier ones to make sure that they succeed and to protect their ego.

To a fixed mindset child, the success of others is seen not as source of inspiration but as a threat. Similarly, feedback which isn't positive can be ignored and excuses can be made for poor performance such as, 'My teacher is useless'. Others may 'explain' away difficulty with a subject by simply saying, 'I'm useless at science' (or practical work or physics equations or whatever).

The times around transition to secondary school and adolescence are very trying for the fixed mindset child. They have to maintain the image of being effortlessly smart and keep any flaws well hidden in order to protect their ego. They see school as a testing place where adults are out to discover their weaknesses. So, to protect themselves, they simply stop trying and retreat into their comfort zone. This defensive withdrawal of effort may explain why some pupils don't push themselves and consequently underperform.

From fixed to growth mindset

What fixed mindset children need is a good dose of meta-cognition. They need to be helped to really reflect on the reasons why they think in the ways they do. They need to see that:

- They have to challenge themselves and that they can do so without damaging their ego.
- Overcoming difficulty will probably involve effort, but this is not a bad thing.
- Above all, they really can develop a growth mindset and that intelligence is not fixed.

They also need to understand that growth mindset children:

- Want to learn from the success of others.
- Embrace challenges.
- Welcome constructive feedback and learn from it.
- See that effort expended to master difficult material will grow their brains and help them to become more intelligent.

Which sort of pupils would you like to have in your classroom or lab? Isn't this worth teaching and constantly reinforcing alongside the learning habits? So, how can you do this?

First, model a growth mindset yourself. Constantly refer to how intelligence and ability are not fixed and that effort grows the brain. Explain the science behind new neural connections in the brain and use analogies like, 'To build and strengthen muscle you need to work out'. For example, in order to move through the levels in computer games you need persistence, the ability to try different strategies and lots of practice and time. So it is when mastering difficult concepts.

Put up motivational posters or logos and regularly refer to them. Pair up growth and fixed mindset pupils. Use successful past pupils as role models and tell stories about famous scientists to reinforce a growth mindset. For instance, Einstein did badly at school and at college. One of his teachers said in a report, 'You will never amount to very much'. Thomas Edison was thrown out of school for being 'educationally subnormal'.

Finally, be very careful about how you use praise – especially in one-to-one situations.

Praise with care

How children develop the mindsets they have about their ability and intelligence is complex, but one factor plays a large part: how children are praised.

Dangerous praise

Dweck found that praising children for their ability when achieving a successful outcome in a task with phrases like, 'Well done. You must be smart,' cultivated a fixed mindset in many of them about the task. So, in order to continue to look smart they would later choose easier rather than harder tasks. But, if children were praised for their effort by saying, 'Wow, you did really well. You must have tried very hard,' they tended later to choose to do the harder tasks.[7]

Try to avoid giving praise like, 'I'm proud of you' or 'You're good at this'. This can reinforce the false assumption that success is due to personal attributes and teaches pupils to interpret difficulties in terms of their personal weaknesses. Try instead to focus praise on the processes, strategies and effort shown by making comments such as, 'That was a good way to do it' or 'Show me how you did it'. This strengthens the notion that effort and the use of effective strategies is rewarding and that difficulties may be due to lack of effort or inappropriate strategies.

Also praise the pupils' work – for example, 'Good diagram. All the labels are correct', 'There are hardly any spelling mistakes this time', 'Good use of terminology'. Never give praise if it is not justified.

Dishonest praise

Always avoid what Willingham (2009: 183) calls dishonest praise: 'Don't praise effort where none exists, it is destructive as pupils see right through it and it leads to you losing credibility.'

---

7   You can see this in action, and hear Carol Dweck discussing it, at: http://www.youtube.com/watch?v=TTXrV0_3UjY.

And as Berger tellingly says:

> 'We can't *first* build the students' self-esteem and then focus on their work. It is through their own work that their self-esteem will grow. I don't believe self-esteem is built from compliments. Students who are struggling or producing lousy work know exactly how poor their performance is – compliments never seem genuine. All the self-esteem activities and praise in the world won't make them feel like proud students until they do something of value.'
>
> Berger (2003: 65)

Hattie and Yates could find no evidence that praise alone can help learning, but of continuous praise they are damning:

'Seriously, if we want to produce people who lack persistence and self-control, who are accustomed to immediate gratification as their default position, then rewarding them on every single opportunity is one known technique. ...

Any such continuous praise violates one of the well entrenched cannons [*sic*] of behavioural psychology: that intermittent and unpredictable reinforcement produces strong and persistent habits, whereas constant and unpredictable reinforcement leads you to stop efforts once reinforcement is no longer present.'

Hattie and Yates (2014: 68)

So, the lesson to learn here is to use praise sparingly and to use it to praise genuine effort, not ability. Additionally, praise pupils' persistence/resilience when undertaking difficult tasks and for taking responsibility for doing the task. Constantly reinforce the message that finding things hard is normal and is simply part of the learning process.

Avoiding labelling and how to praise effort

Avoid labels that judge:

Bright ✗	Clever ✗	Intelligent ✗
Smart ✗	Right ✗	Brilliant ✗
Quick ✗	Greatest ✗	Excellent ✗
Beautiful ✗	Pretty ✗	Cute ✗
Lovely ✗	Amazing ✗	Wonderful ✗
The best ✗	Better than ... (another person) ✗	

Use words that encourage and assist metacognition about learning strategies:

Let's see what you did. ✓   Wow! ✓

Look at that! ✓   Tell me about it. ✓

Show me more. ✓   How did you do that? ✓

How do you feel about it? ✓

That looks like it took a lot of work/effort. ✓

How many ways did you try it before it
turned out the way you wanted it? ✓

What do you plan to do next? ✓

How did you work that out? ✓

Are you pleased with what you did? ✓

Let's try that again. ✓   What is the first step? ✓

Not quite, try ... ✓   Try again with ... ✓

Can you rephrase that by ...? ✓

Avoiding implicit reproach

It is all too easy to say things like, 'That was simple, no one should have got it wrong', 'I'm surprised bright kids like you didn't get it' or 'What? Where did that come from?' Pupils *will* get things wrong in lessons – remind and reassure them that this is a normal part of learning and that to show effort and try is what you value first. No one should sit in a lesson of yours thinking, 'I don't get this', and keep quiet.

Pupils in your classroom or lab should not be afraid to admit defeat or to have a go, because the positive environment that you have fostered makes them feel safe and encouraged by all.

Afterthoughts

I have always thought that science is potentially the hardest subject to learn and to teach. There is a scientific method and a scientific language to learn. There are complex and baffling ideas, most of which involve grasping intangible concepts that require mental gymnastics to appreciate and model. And then there is the sheer quantity of content to grasp. The subject is huge, taking in everything from subatomic particle physics to the vastness of the universe. But the more you learn, the more you see how all that apparently disparate content is actually connected at a fundamental level. There is a beauty in it.

Science is certainly the most important subject taught in school. After all, we learn English to be able to read and write about science, maths so we can do the graphs and calculations, history to learn about the development of scientific ideas and so on. It's true – but don't tell this to colleagues in secondary schools!

More seriously, science is important because it is so fundamental to our daily lives. Without it, and the technologies and engineering it has spawned, we would truly be living in ignorance and literally in the dark.

Science both engages and satisfies our curiosity, but for many of our young people a relentless diet of science teaching to the test has almost extinguished this desire for knowledge. They have lost the big picture; they see science as a disparate jumble of unconnected, soon-to-be-forgotten facts, having little bearing on their lives. We need to reignite their curiosity and re-motivate our young people to meet the challenges of terminal examinations. Not through the endless revision of facts but by deepening their knowledge, thereby allowing them to see the big picture.

To do this we need to be not only creative in how we communicate science but also in how we help our pupils to develop the skills, mindsets and habits of great learners. If we succeed in this, we will produce young people who are independent and resilient and who can learn to adapt and transfer their scientific knowledge to new contexts and tackle the challenges science offers with enthusiasm and real understanding.

Our future depends on it.

Appendix 1

Student Questionnaire

Group: *Teacher:*

Your gender: Male/female (Please circle)   Year group:

Please answer the questions carefully and honestly. For each question, please tick the box which best fits your response. Please ensure your √ fills only one box. Your responses will help your teachers to ensure that we offer you the best opportunities to learn.		1. Always	2. Usually	3. Sometimes	4. Never
1	How often does the teacher share with you what you are going to learn (the content and skills) in a lesson at the start?				
2	How often does the teacher review with you what has been learned in a lesson at the end?				
3	How often do you have the opportunity to problem-solve with others in this lesson?				
4	How often do you have the opportunity to work as a group within this lesson?				
5	How often does the peer assessment you do help you to make progress?				

Please answer the questions carefully and honestly. For each question, please tick the box which best fits your response. Please ensure your √ fills only one box. Your responses will help your teachers to ensure that we offer you the best opportunities to learn.	1. Always	2. Usually	3. Sometimes	4. Never
6	How often are you encouraged to find things out for yourself in this lesson?				
7	How often do you get the opportunity to contribute in this lesson?				
8	Do you know your current level?				
9	Do you know how to get to the next level?				
10	How often are you given the opportunity to review the thinking and learning you have done in this lesson?				
11	How often does the teacher give you the opportunity to give extended answers in this lesson?				
12	How often are you taught to organise your thinking and learning in this lesson?				
13	How often does your teacher help you to make links with other subjects as part of your learning in this lesson?				

Please answer the questions carefully and honestly. For each question, please tick the box which best fits your response. Please ensure your √ fills only one box. Your responses will help your teachers to ensure that we offer you the best opportunities to learn.	1. Always	2. Usually	3. Sometimes	4. Never
14	How often do you have the opportunity to be creative and come up with new ideas and solutions in this lesson?				
15	How often are you encouraged to use a variety of learning strategies and styles in this lesson?				
16	How often do you have the opportunity to try out new ideas in this lesson?				
17	How much of the time in this lesson do you feel really challenged?				
18	How often are you expected to work very hard in this lesson?				
19	How often do you feel supported by the teacher to achieve your very best in this lesson?				
20	How often do you feel supported by your peers to achieve your very best in this lesson?				

Thanks for your help.

Appendix 2

The iSTRIDE Coaching Model

Very briefly, this model suggests that you work with a coach who is supportive and non-judgemental (see Beere and Broughton, 2013: 12–21). The coach acts not as a trainer (telling you what they think you should do) or even as a mentor (advising and guiding). The coach, using non-directive questioning, guides you in as little as ten minutes through the following structured coaching conversation:

I	**Information gathering**
	Determining the coachee's issues, goals, confidence levels and finding relevant evidence.
S	**Strengths**
	Paying attention to the coachee's strengths and maintaining them in a resourceful mindset.
T	**Target/goal-setting**
	Identifying the target to be achieved and exploring the motivation to achieve it.

R	**Resources/reality**
	Exploring the current situation in relation to the target and identifying limiting beliefs.
I	**Ideas/strategies**
	Seeking ideas that might help to achieve the desired target and overcoming limiting beliefs.
D	**Decisions**
	Selecting the most appropriate option from the ideas generated and rehearsing success.
E	**Evaluation**
	There are two parts to this phase: evaluating the solution now (exploring a commitment to agree decisions) and evaluating later (agreeing a time to follow up on the actions taken arising from the decision).

Source: Adapted from Thomas (2005).

Appendix 3
The Solar System

Aim:

To be able to describe the solar system and why the earth has day and night.

1. Find out what the word *orbit* means and in a neat table show how far each planet in our solar system is from the sun.

2. Use the information you found in 1, and a suitable scale, to make a model to show the orbits of the planets.

11. The sun, earth and moon are *approximately spherical bodies.* Note down what this means and be ready to present it to the class.

10. Using a suitable scale, draw the diameters of the sun and the planets.

9. Find a way to use a model of the sun and the rotating earth to explain to the class why we have night and day.

8. What did the scientists named in 7 believe about the solar system?

T
SO
SYS

Work in teams of three or four. Decide who is going to work on each task. You will get credit for neatness and accuracy. Materials and sources of information will be provided.

E AR EM

3. Find out the differences between a *star*, a *planet*, a *dwarf planet* and a *moon*.

4. Find out what a *mnemonic* is. Create one as an easy way of remembering the order of the planets from the sun.

5. Find out the names of ten different moons and show where they are in a table.

6. What is a *geocentric model* and what is a *heliocentric model* of the solar system?

7. Make a table to show when and where these scientists lived: Ptolemy, Alhazen, Galileo and Copernicus.

Appendix 4
The Circulatory System

Group 1. Heart and circulatory system diseases

Tabulate the causes, symptoms and dangers of the following, wherever possible illustrating them with photographs, diagrams, etc.

Aneurysm, angina, arrhythmia, atheroma, cardiovascular disease, excess cholesterol, coronary, hole in the heart, hypertension, myocardial infarction, thrombosis.

You will later present this to the rest of the class.

Group 5. Control of the heartbeat

Prepare an annotated and illustrated flow chart which uses the following terms to describe how the beat is controlled:

Cardiac cycle, autonomic system, vagus nerve, myogenic, septum, atrioventricular node, sinuatrial node, Purkinje fibres, bundle of His, wave of activity.

You will later present this to the rest of the class.

T
circu
sys

Group 4. Design and carry out experiments to investigate:

- Resting pulse rate
- Pulse rate during exercise
- Recovery time
- Arterial elasticity

Include cardiac output.

After trialling these, you will lead the rest of the class in carrying out these investigations.

Aim:

For the whole class to be able to interpret pressure and volume data and ECG traces.

Each group must prepare a 40 minute lesson on your topic to teach the rest of the class.

Group 2. The functions of the mammalian circulatory system

Prepare an illustrated talk on the functions of circulatory systems and the advantages of a double circulatory system over a single circulatory system.

Include prepared dissections, drawings and diagrams to show the structure of these parts: arteries, veins, capillaries, arterioles.

You will later present this to the rest of the class.

Group 3. Heart structure

Prepare pinned and labelled heart dissections and diagrams to show the following:

Atria, ventricles, left and right atrioventricular valves, septum, aorta, pulmonary artery and vein, vena cava and coronary artery.

After preparing these, you will lead the rest of the class in carrying out this dissection.

Appendix 5
Bloom's Taxonomy Verbs

Use verbs aligned to Bloom's Taxonomy to create discussion questions and lesson objectives.

Knowledge

Count	Define	Describe	Draw	Enumerate	Find	Identify
Label	List	Match	Name	Quote	Read	Recall
Recite	Record	Reproduce	Select	Sequence	State	Tell
View	Write					

Comprehend

Classify	Cite	Conclude	Convert	Describe	Discuss	Estimate
Explain	Generalise	Give examples	Illustrate	Interpret	Locate	Make sense of
Paraphrase	Predict	Report	Restate	Review	Summarise	Trace
Understand						

Apply

Act	Administer	Articulate	Assess	Change	Chart	Choose
Collect	Compute	Construct	Contribute	Control	Demonstrate	Determine

Develop	Discover	Dramatise	Draw	Establish	Extend	Imitate
Implement	Interview	Include	Inform	Instruct	Paint	Participate
Predict	Prepare	Produce	Provide	Relate	Report	Select
Show	Solve	Transfer	Use	Utilise		
Analyse						
Break down	Characterise	Classify	Compare	Contrast	Correlate	Debate
Deduce	Diagram	Differentiate	Discriminate	Distinguish	Examine	Focus
Illustrate	Infer	Limit	Outline	Point out	Prioritise	Recognise
Research	Relate	Separate	Subdivide			
Synthesise						
Adapt	Anticipate	Categorise	Collaborate	Combine	Communicate	Compare
Compile	Compose	Construct	Contrast	Create	Design	Develop
Devise	Express	Facilitate	Formulate	Generate	Incorporate	Individualise

Synthesise *cont ...*

Initiate	Integrate	Intervene	Invent	Make up	Model	Modify
Negotiate	Organise	Perform	Plan	Pretend	Produce	Progress
Propose	Rearrange	Reconstruct	Reinforce	Reorganise	Revise	Rewrite
Structure	Substitute	Validate				

Evaluate

Appraise	Argue	Assess	Choose	Compare/contrast	Conclude	Criticise
Critique	Decide	Defend	Evaluate	Interpret	Judge	Justify
Predict	Prioritise	Prove	Rank	Rate	Reframe	Select
Support						

Source: https://www.teachervision.com/tv/printables/misc07/BloomsTaxonomyVerbs.pdf.

Bibliography

Anderson, M. (2013). *Perfect ICT Every Lesson*. Carmarthen: Independent Thinking Press.

Beere, J. (2007). *The Learner's Toolkit: Supporting the SEAL Framework for Secondary Schools*. Carmarthen: Crown House Publishing.

Beere, J. (2011). *The Perfect (Ofsted) Lesson*. Carmarthen: Independent Thinking Press.

Beere, J. (2014). *The Perfect Teacher*. Carmarthen: Independent Thinking Press.

Beere, J. and Broughton, T. (2013). *The Perfect Teacher Coach*. Carmarthen: Independent Thinking Press.

Berger, R. (2003). *An Ethic of Excellence: Building a Culture of Craftsmanship with Students*. Portsmouth, NH: Heinemann.

Berger, R., Rugen, L. and Woodfin, L. (2014). *Leaders of Their Own Learning: Transforming Schools Through Student-Engaged Assessment*. San Francisco, CA: John Wiley & Sons.

Biggs, J. and Collis, K. (1982). *Evaluating the Quality of Learning: The SOLO Taxonomy*. New York: Academic Press.

Department for Education (2013). *Science Programmes of Study: Key Stages 1 and 2. National Curriculum in England*. Ref: DFE-00182-2013. Available at: https://www.gov.uk/government/uploads/system/uploads/attachment_data/file/239132/PRIMARY_national_curriculum_-_Science.pdf.

Dweck, C. S. (2006). *Mindset: The New Psychology of Success*. New York: Ballantine Books.

Elder, Z. (2012). *Full On Learning: Involve Me and I'll Understand*. Carmarthen: Crown House Publishing.

Griffith, A. and Burns, M. (2013). *Outstanding Teaching: Engaging Learners*. Carmarthen: Crown House Publishing.

Gladwell, M. (2005). *Blink: The Power of Thinking Without Thinking*. London: Penguin.

Hattie, J. (2012). *Visible Learning for Teachers: Maximising Impact on Learning*. London: Routledge.

Hattie, J. and Yates, G. (2014). *Visible Learning and the Science of How We Learn*. London: Routledge.

Johnston, H. (2012). 'The Spiral Curriculum' (Research into Practice Brief). Education Partnerships, Inc. Available at: http://gearup.ous.edu/sites/default/files/Research-Briefs/ResearchBriefSpiralCurriculum.pdf.

Lemov, D. (2009). *Teach Like a Champion Field Guide: A Practical Resource to Make the 49 Techniques Your Own*. San Francisco, CA: Jossey-Bass.

Martin, M. O., Mullis, I. V. S., Foy, P. and Stanco, G. M. (2012). *TIMSS 2011 International Results in Science*. Chestnut Hill, MA: TIMSS & PIRLS International Study Center, Boston College.

Nadler, R. T., Rabi, R. and Minda, J. P. (2010). Better Mood and Better Performance: Learning Rule-Described Categories is Enhanced by Positive Mood, *Psychological Science* 21: 1770–1776. Available at: http://www.psych.uncc.edu/pagoolka/seminar/PS2010.pdf.

Ofsted (2011). *Reading, Writing and Communication (Literacy)* (21 October). Ref: 110125. Available at: http://www.ofsted.gov.uk/resources/reading-writing-and-communication-literacy.

Ofsted (2013). *Maintaining Curiosity: A Survey Into Science Education in Schools* (21 November). Ref: 130135. Available at: http://www.ofsted.gov.uk/resources/maintaining-curiosity-survey-science-education-schools.

Bibliography

Ofsted (2014a). *The Framework for School Inspection* (31 July). Ref: 120100. Available at: http://www.ofsted.gov.uk/resources/framework-for-school-inspection.

Ofsted (2014b). *School Inspection Handbook* (31 July). Ref: 120101. Available at: http://www.ofsted.gov.uk/resources/school-inspection-handbook.

Sherrington, T. (2014) *Teach Now! Science: The Joy of Teaching Science.* London: Routledge.

Thomas, W. (2005). *Coaching Solutions Resource Book.* London: Network Continuum Education.

White, N. (2000). High Standards: A Culture of Educational Quality, *Edutopia* (1 October). Available at: http://www.edutopia.org/shutesbury-elementary-school-PBL.

Willingham, D. T. (2009). *Why Don't Students Like School?* San Francisco, CA: John Wiley & Sons.

Wilshaw, M. (2014). HMCI's speech to the North of England Education Conference (15 January). Available at: http://www.ofsted.gov.uk/resources/north-of-england-education-conference-2014-hmci-speech.

978-178135100-0

978-178135137-6

978-178135002-7

www.independentthinkingpress.com